WAYS AND MEANS

A STUDY OF THE ECONOMIC STRUCTURE
OF GREAT BRITAIN TO-DAY

MACMILLAN AND CO., Limited
LONDON · BOMBAY · CALCUTTA · MADRAS
MELBOURNE

THE MACMILLAN COMPANY
NEW YORK · BOSTON · CHICAGO
DALLAS · ATLANTA · SAN FRANCISCO

THE MACMILLAN COMPANY
OF CANADA, LIMITED
TORONTO

WAYS AND MEANS

A STUDY OF THE ECONOMIC STRUCTURE
OF GREAT BRITAIN TO-DAY

TWELVE BROADCAST TALKS

BY

GEOFFREY CROWTHER

MACMILLAN AND CO., LIMITED
ST. MARTIN'S STREET, LONDON
1936

PRINTED IN GREAT BRITAIN
BY R. & R. CLARK, LIMITED, EDINBURGH

PREFACE

The talks printed in this book were broadcast in the National Programme of the B.B.C. on twelve successive Thursday evenings in the last three months of 1935. I have printed them almost exactly as they were delivered. A few introductory, and purely repetitive, paragraphs have been omitted. On the other hand, one or two paragraphs which had to be cut out before broadcasting on the score of time have been included.

The talks were, of course, composed in Spoken English, which is a very different language from Written English. I have altered one or two phrases which would have looked particularly clumsy in print, but I have made no attempt to translate the whole book into the written language. I would ask those who find the style tedious or excessively personal to bear this in mind.

Economists, into whose hands this book may fall, will criticise many of my generalisations, while statisticians will dispute the accuracy of my figures. So let me forestall, if not disarm, criticism, by saying that I deliberately set out to prefer a clear and broadly true argument to an involved and impregnable one, easily grasped round numbers to scientifically accurate statistics. After all, elaborate provisos and decimal points have no place in a dinner-time talk.

This is a convenient opportunity to express my thanks to all those people at the B.B.C. who gave me such courteous assistance, especially to Mr. Roger Wilson and Mr. N. G. Luker. Thanks are also due to the listeners who took the trouble to write to me about the talks. These letters are the most helpful and gratifying response that a broadcast lecturer can receive.

G. C.

HAMPSTEAD
Boxing Day 1935

CONTENTS

ILLUSTRATIONS

1. THE NATIONAL INCOME

It is many years since Carlyle christened economics the "dismal science" and I am afraid that most people probably still consider it a very appropriate description. There are two reasons, in my opinion, for this. The first is the fault of the economists, for they will persist in writing—and sometimes broadcasting—in the most unintelligible way about ordinary common-sense matters. If a man is writing about atomic physics, or palaeontology or radiotherapy, you don't expect to understand him. But when he starts talking about matters that are familiar to all of us—like wages and the price of eggs, rents, rates and taxes—you do expect him to make himself understood. And when, after his unintelligible arguments, he arrives at a conclusion which seems to be contrary to common sense—when he tells you, for instance, that the best way of increasing the income of the working-class is to lower wages—you naturally suspect that there is some jiggery-pokery. I have called this the economist's fault. And so it is, when he does not make himself clear. But it is also his misfortune. For economics is not a simple subject, although it does deal with everyday matters. The psychologists have been much cleverer than the economists, for they have invented very long and scientific-sounding words for the everyday matters with which they deal. They talk of psychoses and neuroses and complexes and introspection, and the ordinary man never guesses that these are all things which are familiar to him under other names. If economists talked about "pecuniary effort-compensations" instead of wages and "valuational factors" instead of prices, they would be forgiven, and even respected, for being unintelligible.

The second reason why economics is regarded as the "dismal science" is that it deals with the financial and industrial system by which we all earn our daily bread. And with two million men and women earning no daily bread, the system is obviously in a pretty dismal state. As a result, most of the economic writing and speaking in the last few years has been concerned with the faults of the economic machine. Some say the machine is all right if only the politicians would let it alone. Others say that the machine is faultily constructed and must be entirely rebuilt. A vast amount of ink and paper and hot air is used by those who claim they have a complete cure and by those who seek to prove that the other people's cure would only make matters worse. And the net result of all the confusion, so far as the ordinary man is concerned, is bewilderment.

Now in this book I am not going to join in the argument about what is wrong with the economic machine: I am going to attempt to explain how the machine works. Some of us forget that the machine is still working. In concentrating on the 2 million unemployed, we forget the 12 or 15 millions who are employed. The economic machine is like a six-cylinder engine which is missing on one cylinder. It is, of course, important that the trouble in that last cylinder should be put right. But it is equally important to know what is going on in the other five. In a sense, machine is the wrong word to use about the system by which we live and work, for a machine necessarily works in the same way from beginning to end. But the economic system is continually evolving, sprouting new cylinders, if you will, and letting others wither. It never stands still, and even in these years of depression and unemployment there have been great changes beneath the surface.

There are 45 million people in the United Kingdom. The great majority are provided, either by their own efforts or through the efforts of others, with food, clothing, housing, the necessaries and the amenities of life. Some have far more than they need, others have far less. But all have something. Where do these goods come from? Where does the nation get its living? What are the ways and means of feeding, clothing and housing a nation of 45 million people?

These are the questions I am setting out to answer. In other words, my purpose is description and explanation. Do not expect me to tell you whether Socialism or Capitalism is right. Even if I knew the answer, it is not the sort of thing I intend to discuss in this book. But both the Socialist and the Capitalist must start with the nation as it is. They must build upon the facts of Great Britain in 1935. I am going to attempt to give you the more important of the facts, to illustrate the changes that are going on in the country and to show where they are leading us. And then, with the facts in hand, it is for you to supply the arguments.

Now for question Number One: How does the nation get its living? And as will be the case with many of our questions, the first step is to see what the question means.

When you and I speak of our income, we know perfectly well what we mean. We mean the pounds, shillings and pence which come to us every week, every month or every quarter. And we also know perfectly clearly what we do with it. We spend it on rent, on food, on clothes, on bus rides, on going to the pictures, on insurance—on a thousand and one different things. Some of it we fully intend to save—and every now and then somebody actually succeeds in putting something by for a rainy day.

But what is the National Income? The *Government* has an income like any of us—so much money raised from the taxpayer and spent on battleships, unemployment assistance payments, and postmen's wages. But the Government is only part of the nation. What is the *nation's* income? Clearly the nation as a whole does not have an income in money. For money is only the means by which individuals can exchange goods of different sorts with one another. You and I may be richer if we have a pile of pound notes. But the nation as a whole would not be a whit better off if there were ten times as many pound notes in existence. You can't eat money or dress in it, or inhabit it. Nothing is inherently so useless as money. And indeed, even in your case or mine, it really isn't the money that constitutes our income—it is the clothes and the bread and the bus rides we can buy with it. Money is only a convenient way of calculating the *size* of income. It is the loaves of bread and the suits of clothes that are the real income.

In exactly the same way, the National Income consists of all the goods which are available for the consumption of the citizens of the nation. Not only goods, however, for there are services to be included. The bread you eat, the clothes you wear, the house you live in, the newspaper you bought this evening—all these things you can see and touch do not make up the total of your income. There are the services of the policeman who protects your home, the services of the postman who delivers your letters, the services of the doctor who attends you when you are ill, the services of the economist who tells you about the National Income—all these are part of your income and you pay for all of them, directly or indirectly. In just the same way, the National Income consists not only of the tangible goods available for the citizens of the nation, but also of the services they perform for each other.

Now this may strike you as a curious proposition—that the postman's knock, the policeman's beat and the broadcaster's talk are all part of the National Income—it sounds a bit like taking in each other's washing. But in truth, it is so. Policemen and postmen get paid for their services—so even do broadcasters—and since they are paid willingly, it may be taken that their services are considered valuable. And as the National Income consists of all the valuable things that are at the nation's disposal, services must be included.

The National Income, then, consists of all the valuable goods and services enjoyed by the citizens of the nation. It is the starting-point of these talks. And the first thing we want to know about it is, where do these goods and services come from? Most of them, obviously, come from the hard work put in by the individuals who compose the nation. The goods produced by British labour, together with the services rendered by British labour, make up the greater part of the income of the country. The nation provides for itself nearly all of what it consumes. Not quite all, however, for some of the goods we consume come from abroad—our food especially—and we have to send to foreign countries some of the goods we produce in payment for the goods we import. In other words, we grow less food than we consume, but, on the other hand, we make more cotton goods, we mine more coal and we build more ships than we need ourselves. Goods are not the only things we send to foreign countries; we also sell them our services. Every time a foreigner pays for his goods to be carried on a British ship, every time he draws upon the skill and experience of British insurance companies, every time he borrows British money, he is paying for a British service.

The nation is, then, a great co-operative organisation for the production of wealth, and the National Income is the sum total of the wealth it contrives to produce in a year. I have used the word co-operative. There are some who do not put into the pool of wealth nearly as much as they draw out. There are others who do not draw out as much as they put in. But the system is co-operative in the sense that each of us depends upon the

B

others. There is not a single family in the United Kingdom to-day which by its own efforts provides all its own wants. Every one of us consumes some goods which somebody else had produced; every one of us is, to some extent, dependent upon services rendered by somebody else. Much the clearest and most helpful way of picturing the economic mechanism of a nation is to think of it as a pool of goods and services to which all contribute and from which all draw.

Now each of us draws very much the same sort of things from the pool. Some like meat and others potatoes—but we all need food. Some live in castles and others in cottages—but we all need house-room. There are differences of detail, but the *sort* of thing we consume does not vary very much from person to person. I suppose that a list of one or two thousand things would cover pretty well all the things the ordinary family ever buys for its own use or enjoyment. The rich buy more of them and finer qualities, the poor have to put up with comparatively few of the cheaper qualities, but the same sorts of things are bought by everybody.

But the ways in which we earn our living show almost endless variations. Think of the people you know who live in the same street and the variety of ways in which they earn a living; look at the people in the bus or train to-morrow morning and try to

THE OCCUPATIONS OF THE PEOPLE, 1931 (figures in millions).

guess what the trade of each one is. You may find
two families living side by side, each consuming
very much the same sort of things—and yet the
bread-winner in one may be a clerk in a city office,
dependent for his living on the ups and downs of
the market in peanuts, while the other earns his
living by making sparking plugs for aeroplane
engines. Even such a comparatively simple thing
as a loaf of bread has required the labour and
services of scores of different trades to make it—
not only the baker, the miller and the farmer, but
makers of ovens and milling machinery and reaping
machines, several different sorts of merchants and
many different varieties of transport workers.
And behind the machinery-makers are all the
trades engaged in making iron and steel, right
back to the miners of coal and iron ore.

Let me put the point in another way. Just ask
yourself how much of your own requirements you
yourself directly provide. It may be that you are a
farmer and you can say that you grow part of your
own food. But even then you are dependent upon
the makers of agricultural implements. It may be
that you are a musician and can provide part of
your own entertainment—provided somebody else
will make a piano or a violin for you. It may be
that you are a builder and have built your own
house—with bricks that somebody else has made,
and windows that were made elsewhere and

timber which somebody else provided. But the chances are that you are none of these things. The chances are that you yourself provide only the tiniest fraction of your requirements—if indeed you provide any at all. Suppose, for example, that you are a machine-tool maker. You have not the slightest personal use for machine-tools. Not one of them ever enters your home—and if it did it would be entirely useless. Nevertheless, your services in making machine-tools are valuable services and form part of the National Income. But they are valuable services only because somebody wants machine-tools in order to make a piece of machinery which in turn will make a small part of the engine of the motor-van which brings the bread round to your door. Your services in making machine-tools are a tiny fraction of the labour and services and materials that have gone into the loaf of bread. But before you can contribute your labour and skill, and before you can assist in making loaves of bread, it is necessary that this whole complicated system of bakers and motor-van makers and engineers and machine-tool makers should be in existence and should be working properly.

We have discovered by experience that a complicated system of this sort is the most efficient. If everybody specialises on one particular job and concentrates on doing that, many more goods will be provided than if every family attempted to provide all its own wants. This is a very old economic principle known as the division of labour, and as time goes on labour gets more and more divided and specialised and the system gets more and more complicated.

How does it happen that the pieces of this very complicated machine all fit together? How does it happen that the machine-tool maker, although his work seems to be so very far removed from the loaf of bread, can yet find employment and wages? Now, of course, one answer is that all the pieces *don't* fit together; there always seem to be some left over for which no use can be found and which have to be supported in idleness by their fellows. But in concentrating on the unfortunate minority, we are far too apt to forget the majority. We are far too ready to forget how very remarkable it is that such a complicated system should work at all. As Dr. Johnson said of the dog that walked on his hind legs: "The remarkable thing is, not that he does it badly, but that he can do it at all!" At the present moment, six out of seven of the pieces of our economic mechanism *do* fit together. And I hope you will not think me complacent when I say that that is a very remarkable achievement for any economic system. It may be that we might be able (and we certainly ought to try) to evolve a system which would work even more efficiently, or which would achieve its results with less injustice between men. That may be, but do not let us underrate the achievements of our present system.

Now obviously a complicated mechanism like this needs regulating and keeping in order, and my next task is to say a word or two about the ways and means of regulating and adjusting the economic system.

But before we do that, we must first ask what we want an economic system to do. I suggest that there are three things we want it to do. First, we want it to produce as many as possible of the goods and services we want—that is, we want it to be *efficient*. Secondly, we want it to adjust itself readily to changes in conditions—we do not want it to go on turning out stage-coaches after railways have been invented; we want it to find different work for cotton spinners who permanently lose their jobs. We can express this by saying that our economic system must be *adaptable*. And, thirdly, we want it to work justly and fairly between man and man, not oppressing one and lifting another undeservedly above his fellows. We want it to be *equitable*. Efficiency, adaptability, equity—these are our three ideals.

Thousands of people have written books about the way in which the economic system should be run. And for every thousand books there are a thousand different opinions. But, broadly speaking, people tend to fall into two main schools of thought. These two schools shade into each other as heat shades into cold, but if I describe the two extreme points of view, you will have a fair idea of the quarrel.

One school of thought says that the only thing necessary is to leave everyone alone, to restrain nobody and assist nobody, to let them do what they want—and this school of thought is known by the French words for "let do"—*laissez-faire*. It is claimed for this system that it is the most *efficient* that could be devised. For if there is a profit to be made out of doing anything, it will be done, and nobody will be deterred by the threat of taxation or by labour laws or by trade-union action from doing what he wants. It is also claimed that it is the most *adaptable* system, for it concentrates on making those things for which people are prepared to pay money. As soon as they no longer want stage-coaches, there will be no profit in making them, so none will be made. And when cotton-spinners are thrown out of work, they will have to lower their wages until they find other work to do and, since the alternative is starvation, they will have to do it quickly. But this *laissez-faire* system does not satisfy the third test—that of *equity*. Since it concentrates on making those things for which most money is offered, it satisfies the needs of the rich rather than those of the poor.

It is possible that complete *laissez-faire* would produce a greater amount of goods and services than any other system. But it is an indefensibly unfair system: it makes the rich richer and the poor poorer.

The other extreme view is the exact opposite— that the Government should plan and regulate everything, allowing no freedom or initiative to anyone, abolishing all profits and subjecting every business to the orders of the State. This system might be more equitable—in fact, it could ordain a complete equality of income, if it chose. But its efficiency would depend upon whether the Government officials and politicians who would be responsible for it could organise the production of goods and services as effectively as it is organised by the private decisions of hundreds of thousands of business men. And the Government officials would not merely have to produce *any* goods and services but the goods and services that people wanted.

We may perhaps conclude that this system would almost certainly not be more efficient than *laissez-faire* and would probably be rather less efficient. What about adaptability? Well, all that we can say is that whenever governments have taken over the running of business, whether it be rubber in Malaya or sugar in Cuba or coffee in Brazil or railways in any one of half a dozen countries, they have always proved themselves most unready and unable to adapt themselves to changing circumstances. This alternative system of State control would, therefore, be fairer than *laissez-faire*, but it would very probably be less efficient and it would almost certainly be less adaptable.

There is, consequently, something to be said for either extreme. I shall not attempt to choose between them—you must argue it out for yourself. I am only concerned to point out that our present system is neither one nor the other. In fact, I venture the guess that our present system is perhaps half-way between the two—perhaps a little nearer to *laissez-faire* than to planning, but there isn't much in it. There are certainly very many things that the business man may not do. He may not pay less than the standard rate of wages; he may not send his goods over national frontiers without paying tariffs; there is a growing number of trades which he may not enter at all. If you do not believe me ask any business man, any employer, if he can do what he wants. But, on the other hand, we are obviously a very long way from complete planning.

The economic system which I shall be describing in this book is thus a mixed one, a compromise. It is changing from year to year as we watch it, and most often the changes are away from *laissez-faire* and towards planning. Whether this is a good thing or not, I leave it to you to judge. There are those who say that we shall be compelled either to turn back towards complete *laissez-faire* or to go forward to complete planning. But for the moment we are in a half-way state, and, like all compromises, it has certain advantages and certain disadvantages. And, like all compromises, it does not fit into a nice logical framework nearly as neatly as either of the extremes.

2. THE OCCUPATIONS OF THE PEOPLE

In the course of history the goods that the average family consumes have grown more and more complicated, but for every new addition to the list of consumable goods there have been at least two new ways of earning a living. This contrast—the comparative simplicity of consumption and the complexity of production—is one of the most striking things about our present system. It was not always so. In the early ages of human history, Man had a number of different wants—shelter, clothing, security, several varieties of food—but there were only two trades or professions, tiller of the soil and hunter. But now, instead of two trades supplying all the goods wanted for consumption, scores of separate trades are required to supply each one of our present requirements. I am not going to spend any time in arguing whether this complexity of modern civilisation is a good thing or a bad thing. Its great advantage is that it produces many more goods than a simple society could. Its great disadvantage is that it forces the individual to earn his living in a narrow, specialised calling which teaches him very little of the world as a whole. Also, since it is a complex system, it is much more liable to get out of order. But for our present purpose these arguments are beside the point. The system might be better if it were even more complex; it might be better if it were more simple. But we must take it as it is. The remaining chapters of this book will be devoted to describing and discussing the complex system by which the community earns its living and the more simple, but still very complicated, way in which it spends it. We shall come to the spending side later. For the present we shall be concerned with the ways of earning a living.

I have probably said enough about the complicated nature of the economic system in which we live to convince you that I cannot possibly attempt to give you a list even of the different *sorts* of ways in which people earn their living. But it is possible nevertheless to make certain dividing lines and distinguish certain broad classes of occupations which we can usefully discuss.

The first major distinction we can make is between people who earn their living by making, or helping to make, actual goods which can be seen and handled, and people who earn their living by performing services of one kind and another. We cannot say exactly what the proportion is, but at least half, and possibly more, of all the people who are at work in this country to-day earn their living not by making things, but by performing services.

Perhaps it would be as well to make it quite clear just what is the distinction between making things and performing services. Nothing in this world is created out of nothing, everything had some source, some origin, some raw material. Perhaps we can most easily define "making goods" by saying that it is changing the form or nature of some object. Planting seed in the earth so that it grows into corn, converting grass into meat by breeding cattle, turning cotton fibre into cloth or sheep's fleece into suits, combining coal and iron to make steel, fashioning the steel into various forms, assembling wireless sets—all these and thousands and thousands of other operations change the form of the seed, the wool, the iron, the glass, the wood or whatever it may be. Anybody whose work plays a part in any operation of this sort is helping to make goods. On the other hand, when goods are made, there is a great deal to be done to them. They must be moved from place to place, they must be bought and sold. When a car is moved from Coventry to London, when it is sold by Jones and bought by Smith, its nature is not changed. Moreover, there are millions of people whose daily work never brings them into contact with goods at all. They earn their living by writing or talking or doing sums, or teaching other people to do sums, by cutting other people's hair or curing their diseases. All these are services. Do not be misled into thinking that the difference between making goods and performing services is the difference between manual labour and non-manual labour. There are many men whose manual labour is very arduous—coal-heavers, for example—who are nevertheless to be classified as performing services. This distinction between goods and services is of some practical importance, as I shall show shortly. For the moment I am merely recording the fact that with every year that passes, fewer people earn their living by making goods and more by performing services.

To most people this is a very surprising fact. Through countless centuries of Man's existence, work has been virtually synonymous with manual labour, with making or growing things. Since Adam delved and Eve span, the great majority of men and women have been burdened with growing food, making clothes or toiling laboriously with their hands. Most of us retain an instinctive belief that making things is the only form of work which really creates wealth. Very few people realise that making things now provides a living for only a minority of our people. All the goods you consume, the food you eat, the clothes you wear, the house you live in, the car you drive in, the books you read, every tangible object in your home—all these things are made by only about one-third of the workers, that is, by about one-sixth of the total population of the country. All the rest of us are either dependent on others for our living, or else earn it by performing services of one kind or another, by transporting goods from one place to another, by buying and selling goods or by performing various kinds of personal services.

Now this, when you come to think of it, is a sign of a very high stage of development. In the Middle Ages nearly the whole of the resources of the country had to be devoted to the provision of the bare necessities of life. Almost the whole population, women as well as men, had to work for almost the whole of their waking hours to provide the minimum of food, clothes and shelter. Almost the only services the country could afford were those of the priests and monks, who united in themselves virtually all the professions. It was only very gradually that the other forms of services evolved. Every man who devoted his time to buying and selling, to the law, the church or medicine was one less man to work in the fields. The professions consequently only became possible as the efficiency of agriculture increased; that is, as one man working on the land came to be able to grow food for more than his own family. Gradually the various village crafts grew up—the tinkers and tailors and candlestick makers. And then, as communications improved, trade increased—that is, the exchange of goods with other parts of the country or with foreign countries. And finally, the Industrial Revolution and the discovery of the machine released still more men from making things. Broadly speaking, the more advanced a country is, the greater will be the proportion of its people engaged in performing services rather than in making goods. And there is every reason to believe that in Great Britain the proportion of people making goods will in future fall still lower than it is at present. As time goes on, we shall have to devote less and less of our resources to making things, we shall devote more and more of our resources to travel, education, entertainment, reading and the like. The man who works in a factory weaving cloth or making nuts and bolts is no longer the typical worker; he is in a minority. His place as the type has been taken by the clerk, the lorry-driver, the shopkeeper.

This, then, is the first distinction that we can draw—between the makers of goods and the performers of services. It is a distinction of very great practical importance, to which we shall return in due course. But we must now pass on to the second great distinction. A service must be performed now or never. When you have your hair cut, it is finished and done with. The service of the hairdresser cannot be put into a cupboard and stored

c

until next week. A service, we can therefore say, is consumed at the same moment that it is produced. Now this is true of some goods. A pound of butter, for example, has to be consumed almost at once or else it is useless. A loaf of bread has to be eaten in a comparatively short time or not at all. A newspaper is interesting to-day, but as dull as ditch water to-morrow. But it is not true of all goods. Some of them, wheat for example, can be stored for a considerable time before they are used. And there are other varieties of goods which *cannot* be used quickly. A house, for instance, is not finished and done with when it has been lived in one day, or one month or one year. It gives privacy, warmth and shelter from the elements for many decades.

This is another important distinction. Some goods last a long time, others are used up almost at once. The first we can, for convenience, call *capital* goods, the others *current* goods. The word capital is used in a great many senses, many of them often intended to be derogatory. So perhaps it is as well to explain that by capital goods I mean merely goods which are useful over a long period of time, in contrast to current goods which are consumed immediately, or almost immediately, they are produced. This is one of the most important distinctions in the whole of economics and we shall be coming back to it time and time again.

But let me give you here just one instance of its importance. Current goods, just because they have to be consumed fairly quickly, are always in demand. However severe the slump, men and their families must eat, they must buy a minimum of clothing. But the consumption of capital goods may be entirely postponed. If times are very bad, the production of houses, machinery and other capital goods may stop altogether. However unsatisfactory a house may be, it will nearly always stand for another year or two. Accordingly, employment in those industries which make current goods is much more regular than employment in those industries which make capital goods.

We have then three main classes of workers— those who produce capital goods, those who produce current goods and those who perform services. There are two more main classes which must be included. The first of these consists of those people who earn their living by exporting goods or services; that is, by giving them to foreigners in return for foreign goods and services.

The last of our five classes hardly needs any explanation. It consists of the unemployed—those who for the time being cannot find any work to do.

These, then, are the five classes:

> People who make current goods,
> People who make capital goods,

MAIN CATEGORIES OF WORKERS

24% MAKING CURRENT GOODS (e.g. FOODSTUFFS)

8% MAKING CAPITAL GOODS (e.g. BUILDINGS)

40% SERVICE OF VARIOUS KINDS

14% WORKING FOR EXPORT

14% UNEMPLOYED

EXPORT

V.I.D.I.

People who perform services,
People who make goods or perform
    services for sale to foreigners, and
The unemployed.

It is unfortunately not possible to say exactly how many people there are in each class, and I can only give you a very rough guess. But for what it is worth, my estimate is this: Out of every hundred workers in the country at present, about twenty-four earn their livings by making current goods, about eight by making capital goods, forty by performing services of various kinds, fourteen by making goods or performing services for export and the remaining fourteen are unemployed. Now please remember that these are very rough estimates, designed only to give you some idea of the size of the different classes. Or put it this way— out of every dozen people, the largest group, a little less than five of them, are the service performers. The next largest, with three people, are the makers of current goods. The exporters and the unemployed are almost two each, and the capital goods makers are only one in every twelve. If you add up those figures you will find they come to a baker's dozen of thirteen, but that will just show you how rough the calculation is.

It is unfortunate that there are no precise figures to illustrate this fivefold division of the workers of the country. The only one of the five classes for which we can give a precise figure is that of the unemployed, and that figure, as you know, is announced every month. Perhaps some day, when the census is being taken, people will be asked whether they earn their livings by making things or by performing services. It would certainly be of great value to have those figures.

But in the meantime the only figures we have refer to the *industries* in which people earn their livings. Now this is not the same thing as the division between goods and services. For example, if you are told that there are half a million people in the building trades, that does not mean that they are all engaged in building houses. It includes all the clerks, the designers, the salesmen and the great variety of people who sit in offices. As everybody knows, the proportion of people who sit in offices is increasing in nearly every trade.

But the figures of people working in the different trades nevertheless tell us several very interesting things about the changes that are going on in industry. Every ten years, after the census figures have been collected, the Registrar-General works out what proportion of all the workers is in each particular industry. The last census in this country was taken in 1931. Let us, therefore, take the figures of the 1931 census and compare them with the figures of the 1911 census, just before the war. Of twenty-one different industrial groups, fourteen show an increase in the proportion of the total of workers they employ; the remaining seven show declines. Two-thirds of our industries are expanding; one-third contracting. The big industries are shrinking, the little industries growing.

One of the largest declines is in agriculture and fisheries. In 1911 seventy-seven men and women out of every thousand earned their livings in farming and fishing. In 1931 the figure was only fifty-six in every thousand. One man out of every four has left the farms and the fishing-boats since the period just before the war. Another large decline is even more interesting. It is in the textile, clothing and leather trades, which employed 142 men and women out of every thousand in 1911, but only 111 in 1931.

Why was this? How has it come about that there are so many fewer people earning their living by making cloth and clothes? One of the reasons is that a large part of our export trade in cloth has been lost. But this is not the chief reason, for the clothing trades (*i.e.* those making clothes out of cloth), which have never done very much exporting, show an even larger decline than the textile trades (*i.e.* those making cloth), which have always been very largely dependent upon export trade. The chief explanation is undoubtedly to be found, in my opinion, in the fact that we are not spending nearly as much money on clothes as we used to. In the last twenty years clothes have become standardised. They are made in large factories in large quantities. The thousands of small tailors and dressmakers are gradually going out of business. And, of course, it takes many fewer people to make a thousand suits of clothes in a factory than to make them one by one. In addition, some of us, especially the women, are now wearing very much fewer clothes than we did twenty years ago. As a result of all these changes, we can now make all the clothes and shoes we want with only four-fifths of the workers that were formerly needed.

When we turn to the other great necessity of existence, however—food and drink—we find a rather different state of affairs. We have already seen that there has been a great decline in the number of people employed in agriculture. This was due to at least three causes: first, the increasing efficiency of the agricultural industry, which makes it possible to grow larger crops with fewer men; secondly, the fact that between 1911 and 1931 British farmers were increasingly turning over from crops which require a lot of labour, such as wheat, to livestock breeding and dairy farming, which require comparatively little labour; and, thirdly, because we were buying more of our food from abroad, so fewer men were needed to grow food at home. But, curiously enough, the food and drink *industries*—that is, the industries that cook and pack and manufacture the food that the farmer has grown—show an *increase* in labour from $29\frac{1}{2}$ in every thousand to $32\frac{1}{2}$ in every thousand. The drink industries—brewing and distilling—on the whole employ fewer men, since the consumption of beer and spirits is diminishing. The tobacco industry, on the other hand, employs many more people than it did twenty years ago—there has been a great increase in the cigarette habit, especially since the war, and particularly among the women. But apart from drink and tobacco, the food industries proper have also been increasing. Why is this? Can it be that we are eating more food? Of some sorts we certainly are eating more; but I doubt if we are, as a nation, eating more food of all sorts. The explanation is, I think, to be found in the fact that the preparation of food, which used to be done entirely at home, is now being increasingly done in factories. How many families used to bake their own bread before the war and now buy it from the baker? How much has your own consumption of tinned foods increased in the last twenty years? If you are anything like the average it must have increased very considerably. For all these reasons, an increasing proportion of the workers are earning their living by preparing other people's food.

These, then, are some of the interesting lessons to be derived from the figures of the census of occupations. We employ fewer men and women in making our clothes and in growing our food, but more in actually cooking and preparing food. What other lessons are there to be found? There is, for example, a very large increase in the number of people making electrical apparatus—which of course includes wireless sets. In fact this is the largest increase in the list. And there is a correspondingly large increase in people engaged in generating electricity. The manufacture of vehicles (which means mainly motor-cars) is another industry that shows a large increase. And chemicals is another. These increases are all the natural results of the inventions of the last few decades. But two other increases in the list are interesting for entirely different reasons. The first is paper-making and printing, which shows an increase from $17\frac{1}{2}$ to $22\frac{1}{2}$. This is a reflection, of course, of the very rapid spread of the ability and the desire to read. It is the economic effect of universal education. The second is an increase from 7 to $9\frac{1}{2}$ per thousand in the number of people earning their living in different branches of the entertainments industry. These two increases—in reading and in entertainment—would not have been possible if it had not been for the great reductions in the hours of work which were secured at the end of the war and which, for the great majority of the people, gave the word "leisure" an entirely different meaning. The last increase that I am going to mention is also very significant: a very large increase in the number of people employed by the State, the largest increase being, not, as you might imagine, in Whitehall—that is, the employees of the central government—but in the employees of local authorities, who have increased by more than half in twenty years.

How far are all these changes due to labour-saving machinery? And in particular, how far is labour-saving machinery to blame for unemployment? These are large questions upon which nearly everybody has an opinion—and usually a very definite opinion.

First of all, has labour-saving machinery been introduced faster during the last ten or twenty years than previously? The answer seems to be that there has been very little change. It is a lengthy and not very precise calculation with which I will not bore you now. But the evidence seems to show that the average efficiency of labour—that is, the number of goods and services which the average man, helped by the machine, can turn out—has been increasing for fifty years or more at about 2 per cent each year, and that it is still increasing at about that rate. If anything, it is increasing rather more *slowly* than before—that is, *fewer* labour-saving machines are introduced than before. I think there may be a reason for this. I pointed out a few pages back that over half of our working population earns its living nowadays by performing services rather than by making goods. Now there are some machines which save the labour of service-performers—accounting machines, for example. But the great majority of inventions are new ways of *making things*, and it is very hard to conceive of inventions which would dispense with the services of, say, doctors or lawyers or postmen or shop assistants. As for policemen, inventions seem merely to increase their work. So there is some reason, I suggest, for believing that as fewer and fewer of our people are engaged on making goods, the scope for labour-saving machinery will get smaller and smaller.

Secondly, does labour-saving machinery cause unemployment? I think the only answer to that is that sometimes it does and sometimes it doesn't. In the coal-mining industry, to take one example, there has been a considerable increase in labour-saving machinery. And as a result there are undoubtedly fewer jobs for miners. But in the motor-car industry, to take another example, although it takes many fewer men to make a car now than ten years ago, there are many more men employed.

Well, which is typical—coal-mining or motor-cars—and which is the exception? To that question it is, I think, possible to give a quite definite answer. If machines are, on the whole, displacing men, we should find the production of goods going up while employment goes down. But in point of fact they both go up and down together. Furthermore, if you examine the list of industries, you will find that, with the exception of coal-mining, all those in which there has been most progress in labour-saving machinery are employing more men than they did ten years ago. On the whole, then, the facts seem to point to the conclusion that labour-saving machinery does *not* cause unemployment.

You may not agree with that view. You are, of course, perfectly entitled to believe the contrary. But if you do, take care that your views are in accordance with the hard facts.

3. THE CONTRIBUTION OF FOREIGN TRADE

In the last chapter I divided up the workers of the country, other than the unemployed, into four classes: those making capital goods, such as houses or machinery; those making current goods, such as bread or shirts or gas; those performing services of all kinds; and, lastly, those making goods for export to foreign countries. Two of these classes are large and numerous. The people who perform services and the people who make current goods—goods that have to be used up quickly—together form the largest part of the workers of the country. These two classes between them contain about three-quarters of all the employed workers in the country, leaving only one-quarter for the two small classes—the makers of capital goods—goods that last a long time—and the makers for export. So there are two large classes and two small classes.

You may have been wondering what is the point of this elaborate division into classes. Well, you will see the point just as soon as we begin looking into the identity of the unemployed, and enquiring what class they would belong to if they were not out of work, because a very remarkable fact emerges. The two large classes—current goods

CURRENT GOODS   SERVICES   CAPITAL GOODS   EXPORT

6%   6%   30%   40%

APPROXIMATE PROPORTION OF UNEMPLOYED

IN THE DIFFERENT CLASSES OF WORKERS

and services—have very little unemployment. I
should say at a guess that only about one man in
twelve in these two classes is unemployed. But in
the other two classes—the two small classes—four
men out of twelve are out of work. The two big
classes—current goods and services—have three-
quarters of the workers but little more than one-
third of the unemployed. The two small classes—
capital goods and exports—have one-quarter of the
workers and nearly two-thirds of the unemployed.
Please don't take these figures too literally. They
are only intended to be rough estimates. But they
show what is by far the most important fact to be
grasped about unemployment in Great Britain.
We all of us know that there are depressed *areas*
of the country. We most of us know that there are
depressed *industries* in the country. The point I
am trying to bring out is that the depressed industries are those which fall into the two smallest
of my four classes. They are the industries which
make capital goods and the industries which
sell their products overseas. If we can solve unemployment in these two classes of industries we
shall have broken the back of the unemployment
problem as a whole.

Obviously the easiest way, if it could be done,
would be a revival of activity in the capital goods
and export trades. The unemployed would then be
re-employed at their old jobs near their present

homes. There would be no need to train them to new trades or to move them to new districts. There would then be no need for transfer, no pulling up of roots. It may not be possible, but let us at least enquire why it is that these two branches of industry have declined. If we can find the causes, we may be able to suggest a cure. I shall come back to the capital-goods trades later. For the remainder of this chapter I shall attempt to enquire into the causes of the decline of the export trade.

Perhaps it is a necessary preliminary to ask why we have any foreign trade at all. Part of the answer is obvious. Many of the things we need, either for the consumption of our population or as raw materials for our industries, have to come from abroad because we do not have them at home. All our coffee, our tea, our oranges and lemons, most of our wheat, a fair proportion of our meat or butter—these are examples of imports that the British consumer needs. Our industries are perhaps even more dependent upon imported raw materials—our cotton, wool, iron ore, copper and many other metals, petroleum and other oils and a vast range of materials which we cannot provide at home. Great Britain was blessed by Nature with abundant supplies of coal—but coal is almost the only natural resource of which we have a sufficient supply for all our needs to-day. The rest have to be imported.

D

Imports, of course, have to be paid for. So that we have to sell goods and services to foreigners in order to get the foodstuffs and raw materials we need. And that means that a certain proportion of our workers have to be devoted to making goods and performing services for foreigners.

So far foreign trade is not merely advantageous, it is necessary. But we have gone in the past, and we still go to-day, much further than that. We buy from abroad many things that *could* be made at home. We buy, for example, much wheat, much butter, many eggs, a great deal of bacon that could be grown at home. We buy iron and steel, motor-cars, machinery of many sorts and varieties, although we make all these things at home. Now there are two schools of thought about this. One school of thought says that we should buy from abroad whatever we can get more cheaply in that way than by making or growing it at home. Just as the carpenter concentrates on carpentry and does not spend any of his time in growing food or sewing clothes or making motor-cars, so nations will find that it pays them best for each to concentrate on what it can do best. We in Great Britain could beat the world at coal mining and making cotton and woollen goods, ships and machinery. Therefore, we should make these things for all the world and take payment in the foodstuffs and the raw materials we needed and the manufactures on which other nations concentrated.

This is the Free Trade argument. The other school of thought has, as you know, many arguments on the other side, not the least effective of which is that the other nations of the world have never seen the matter in the same light, and while they have always been ready to *sell* us goods, they have frequently been much less willing to *buy* our goods in return. But it would be contrary to the whole intention of this book if I were to stop here and argue whether Free Trade or Protection is right. The point for us to observe at present is that until the last few years Free Trade was the official policy of Great Britain. During the decades when our economic structure was taking its shape the British public was free to purchase its requirements in the cheapest market, whether that cheapest market was at home or abroad. The result was that something like two-fifths of all the goods consumed in the country came from abroad. And since those imports had to be paid for, and our income from foreign investments was not nearly large enough for the purpose, nearly a third of all our workers had to be employed in making goods or performing services for export. Nearly all our great industries—cotton, wool, coal, steel, engineering, shipbuilding, shipping—were very largely dependent upon export trade. The only large exception was building, which could not, in the

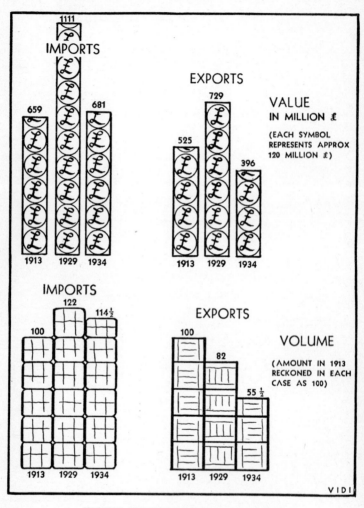

VOLUME AND VALUE OF FOREIGN TRADE

nature of things, make for export.

Before the war this may, or may not, have been the best system for England. The point is that it *was* the system in existence and that it *did* work. But since 1914 it has ceased to work nearly as perfectly as it used to. The business of selling goods abroad and buying foreign goods in exchange has fallen off very sadly, and those who used to earn their living by it are by far the largest contingent in the ranks of the unemployed. Why is it that our export trade has never recovered from the war?

In 1919, just after the Armistice, the trade of the whole world was completely disorganised. But while the trade of other countries picked up in the succeeding years and some of them did better than they had ever done before, British trade never got back to its pre-war level. Our exports, for example, even in the best post-war year, were only 80 per cent of their 1913 amount. That missing 20 per cent represented the jobs of about seven hundred thousand men and women.

There were three main reasons for this comparative failure of British trade. The first was that British exports in the pre-war era had consisted very largely of a few comparatively simple commodities produced by the great staple industries. In fact, in 1913 four goods alone—coal, cotton goods, woollen goods and steel—made up more than half of all our exports. But when, after the war, foreign countries began to protect their own industries and reduce their purchases from abroad, it was precisely these simple staple goods which they started to make for themselves. It is true that they couldn't mine coal if they had no coalfields, but many countries had water-power resources which they could develop in substitution for coal. Cotton and wool are comparatively simple industries to start. Steel is not so simple, but the enormous pressure for munitions during the war had led to a mushroom growth of steel industries in many countries which did not have them before the war.

This meant that the great staple goods in which we had specialised before the war became drugs on the market after the war. The other goods did not do so badly. In 1932, for example, the value of the coal, cotton, wool and steel we sold to foreign countries was only just over half what it had been in 1913. But our sales of all other goods were only about 15 per cent lower than in 1913. So the first reason was just that we were unlucky—that we happened to specialise in producing just those goods which the world decided after the war it would rather make for itself than buy from us. I don't think, however, we can entirely excuse ourselves by pleading bad luck, because we have been far too stubborn in clinging to these out-dated forms of trade. We have been a little inclined to sit down and wait for the world to want our coal and cotton and steel, instead of busying ourselves to supply the newer and more complicated things such as motor-cars, intricate machinery, artificial silk and manufactured foodstuffs which foreign countries *were* willing to buy.

This is reason number one for the decline in British exports—that the nature of world trade had changed and we had not changed with it. Reason number two is that we deliberately made it more difficult to sell our goods by pushing the pound up to an excessively high level. Of course, we didn't *intend* to handicap the export trades, but that was the effect. The whole matter is difficult, and there is no point in adding unnecessary complications at this point by attempting to explain it in full. But the long and the short of it is that by going back to the gold standard in 1925 at a rate of exchange that was more than the pound was really worth our prices and costs were made higher than those of the rest of the world. Consequently our exporters found it difficult to compete successfully in the world's markets and the volume of our exports was reduced accordingly.

The third reason is something of a paradox, and therefore perhaps more difficult to understand. The goods we export to other countries are sent out to pay for the goods we import from them.

And it follows that if we do not have to pay so much for the goods we import, we shall not have to send so many of our goods out to pay for them. Now this is what has happened. The goods we buy, especially the foodstuffs, have been, all through the post-war period, relatively cheaper than before the war. The result is that we have been able to pay for them with fewer of our own goods. In 1929, for instance, which was the best year since the war, we bought from abroad a quarter *more* goods in quantity than in 1913, and paid for them with a fifth *less* of our own goods. From one point of view this was a great gain to Great Britain. It meant that we were getting more from foreign countries and giving them less in return. Every unit of British exports would buy one-third more of foreign goods than before the war. But from another point of view it was not so good, for it meant that one worker out of five in the export industries was no longer needed. In theory he could transfer to another job and contribute his share to the National Income in some other way. But, in practice, when cotton-spinners and coal-miners are no longer needed in the mills or in the mines, it is a very difficult job indeed to transfer them to some other occupation.

These are the three reasons that explain the poor showing that British foreign trade made for the ten years after the war—the slump in the great staple industries, the excessive value given to the pound and the very low prices of imported food-stuffs and raw materials which prevented foreigners from buying as much of our goods as they used to. In the last five years, since 1929, one of these three causes has ceased to operate. The pound came off the gold standard four years ago and since then has been free to find its own level. Indeed, Great Britain has done rather better than other nations in recent years. There is not very much comfort in that, however, for although our slice of the world-trade cake has been growing, the cake itself has been getting very much smaller. All over the world trade has been shrinking most alarmingly. The root cause of this has been the breakdown of the international monetary system, which I shall try to explain in a later chapter. But there is one very remarkable thing to notice about British foreign trade in the last five years. We are still buying very nearly as much stuff from abroad as in 1929—as many pounds of butter or of meat, as many bushels of barley and maize, as much tobacco and rubber—but it is costing us very much less because of the fall in prices. In the case of exports, on the other hand, we have reduced our prices comparatively little, but the volume of goods we sell has fallen off very rapidly—and that means the volume we make, and that means the number of men the export industries employ. We are *buying* the same quantity of goods at lower prices. We are *selling* a smaller quantity of goods at almost the same prices as before. One unit of British exports now buys more than half as much again of foreign goods as it did in 1913.

It is worth pausing a moment to consider what this means. It means two things. First, it means that we have been getting our imported food very cheaply. The farmers have suffered from that, of course, but the great majority of the population has gained immeasurably from the fact that it has been able to go through these hard times with cheap food. Great Britain is the only large country whose consumption of food has *increased* during the depression. We owe that entirely to cheap foreign food. But the second thing that cheap imports mean is that thousands of the workers in the export trades are thrown out of work. Since foreign countries will sell us their goods so cheap, we need to employ fewer men in making goods to send in return. All this is expressed in the technical language of the economist by saying that "the terms of trade have altered to the advantage of Great Britain", but it is a misleading phrase, since the advantage has been very mixed. What has actually happened has been a very considerable gain to the consuming mass of the population at the expense of the farmers and the workers in the export industries. The housewife has gained by getting her food at a lower price. The farmer has lost because the competition of this cheap foreign food has been ruinous. The export worker has lost because the foreigner has been unable to buy the goods he makes.

It is not easy to calculate whether the gain has outweighed the loss or not. The individual farmer or export worker has lost very much more than the individual housewife has gained. But there are many millions more housewives than farmers and export workers put together. Does a small gain to each of twenty million people outweigh a large loss to each of four or five million people?

My task in this book is to expound facts and illustrate them rather than to draw conclusions or advocate policies. But it is impossible to leave the subject of foreign trade without saying something about its future. So much of our unemployment has been caused by the decline of foreign trade and so much of it can be cured quickly only by a revival of foreign trade that it is of supreme importance to enquire what chance there is of a revival. There is another reason—so much nonsense is habitually talked about foreign trade that can quite easily be disproved by looking at a few of the facts.

Take first of all the statement, which one frequently hears, running something like this:

Foreign trade was all right before the war, but the system has now broken down and we can't afford to buy foreign goods. Now it is perfectly true that the system has broken down—but not because we can't afford to buy foreign goods. On the contrary, as I have tried to show, one of the difficulties has been that we have been getting our imports too cheaply. This will not last, of course. Overseas countries will not for ever be content to sell us their wheat and meat and butter below the cost of production. When we have to pay more for our imports, we shall have to send out more goods in payment, and we shall have to employ more men in making them.

Another fallacy which is very widespread runs something like this: Foreign trade worked all right, so long as the rest of the world consisted of backward agricultural areas. But they are now learning to make manufactured goods for themselves, and there is, consequently, no room for British goods. Now there is a germ of truth in this. It is true that foreign countries are beginning to make the simpler things, like cotton cloth, for themselves. They buy less British cotton cloth. But that does not mean that they will buy less British goods of all sorts, if only we have the sense to offer them the goods they want. Moreover, this can be proved with the utmost ease.

Let us take, for example, British trade with

India and compare it with British trade with
Germany. India is an undeveloped, overwhelm-
ingly agricultural country. Germany is almost as
industrial as we are. If there is any truth at all in
the theory that as nations develop their own industries they buy less British goods, you would
expect to find the average Indian buying far more
from us than the average German. In point of fact,
however, in 1934 the German bought nearly twice
as much from us as the Indian. And this was in
1934, when Germany was using every manner and
means of restriction to cut down her purchases of
foreign goods. Or if you think Germany and India
are too far apart to be compared, consider these
facts. Austria and Hungary are two small nations
living side by side in Central Europe. Austria is
industrial, Hungary agricultural. But the average
Austrian, in spite of all his own industries, buys
three times as much from us as the average
Hungarian. Industrial Japan buys three times as
many British goods per head of the population as
agricultural China. The truth is that as these
agricultural nations start building up their own
industries and increasing their own wealth, they
buy *more* British goods, not less. We ought not to
be frightened of industrialisation in other countries. We ought to welcome it with open arms and
cries of joy.

There is another fallacy about international

trade which only needs to be mentioned for its absurdity to be obvious. People sometimes say that whenever you buy anything from abroad that you could have bought at home, you are putting a British workman out of work. This, of course, is pure unadulterated nonsense. Indeed, if it were not for the goods we buy from abroad, there would be many many thousands more unemployed than there are. When you buy Canadian wheat or New Zealand butter or Australian wool or Argentine meat or Danish bacon, you are providing work for somebody in the British steel industry or in British shipping or in some other export industry.

Our brief survey of the plain facts of foreign trade thus suggests two conclusions: First, an increase in foreign trade would be highly desirable, as the most efficacious method of reducing unemployment. Second, there is no inherent reason why British exports should not increase again, when the present crisis is surmounted.

But, of course, that is not the end of the story. Because a thing is desirable and possible doesn't make it likely to happen. I will suggest just two things which will be necessary before a revival of foreign trade can come about, and leave it to you to discuss how they can be done. First, the nations of the world will have to lower all the fantastic barriers and obstructions to trade that have been erected in the past five years. How will you persuade, or compel, them to do that? And second, British exporters will have to offer the world the things it wants—they will have to let the world know that Britain has more things to sell than coal, cotton and steel. How, once more, can we do that?

4. INDUSTRY AND TRADE

A LARGE part of the last chapter was taken up with analysing the formidable total of 2 million unemployed men and women, trying to find out what sort of industries were responsible for this mass of unemployment. In this chapter I want to approach the problem from rather a different angle. Instead of asking what *industries* the unemployed are in, I am going to ask what *districts* they are in. And perhaps the other side of that question is even more interesting. Which parts of the country are prosperous and expanding? and why?

The figures about the geographical distribution of unemployment are easy to come by—they are published every month by the Ministry of Labour —but I am constantly surprised that the very remarkable facts they reveal are so little appreciated. The Ministry of Labour divides Great Britain up into eight geographical divisions, north-east England, north-west England, south-east England, south-west England, London, the Midlands, Scotland and Wales. These divisions are, of course, of varying sizes, so that the only accurate way of comparing them is to contrast the *percentage* of unemployment in each of them.

A certain amount of unemployment is inevitable, even in the most prosperous periods. There are always men changing from one job to another, and unless you assume that they march straight from one job to another, they will be unemployed for brief periods in between. Moreover, there are always some industries which are shrinking and others that are expanding—at least, it would be a most unhealthy state of affairs if that were not so—and this again will cause unemployment. There is, then, a certain minimum of unemployment at all times. And since it is always there we may perhaps call it *normal* unemployment. But this, of course, is a very different thing from the mass unemployment that we have had since the war. When we speak about the unemployment problem, we do not mean what I have called normal unemployment, that is, men out of work temporarily *en route* from one job to another. We mean the hundreds of thousands of men out of work because something has gone wrong with the working of the economic machine. We do not mean normal unemployment, we mean abnormal unemployment. So I am going to try to distinguish between the two. Looking back over the records of the last fifty years, I think that a fair figure for *normal* unemployment would be 4 per cent of the total workers. This means that if the economic system were working as well as it could reasonably be expected to, 96 men and women out of every hundred would be in work, and only 4 would at any time be out of work for any reason, ill-health, incompetence, seasonal slackness or on their way from one job to another. Four per cent is a very small proportion, and I don't think we can put normal unemployment any lower than that.

If 4 per cent is a fair figure for normal unemployment, anything above 4 per cent represents abnormal unemployment. Accordingly, I have subtracted 4 per cent from the figures for each of the geographical divisions of Great Britain, in order to show how much abnormal unemployment each division is suffering from. Here are the figures for August 1935:

The London division had	$3\frac{3}{4}$ per cent of abnormal unemployment			
South-east	,,	$2\frac{1}{2}$	,,	,,	,,
South-west	,,	5	,,	,,	,,
Midlands	,,	$7\frac{1}{2}$	,,	,,	,,
North-east	,,	$16\frac{1}{2}$	,,	,,	,,
North-west	,,	$15\frac{1}{2}$	,,	,,	,,
Scottish	,,	16	,,	,,	,,
Welsh	,,	26	,,	,,	,,

These figures tell a most remarkable story. Four of the divisions have comparatively low figures; let us call them the "good" divisions: they are London, the south-east, the south-west and the Midlands. The other four have comparatively high figures; they are the "bad" divisions: the north-east, the north-west, Scotland and Wales.

Now the extraordinary thing is this: not that the "bad" divisions are worse than the "good" divisions—everybody knows that—but that they are *so much* worse. You might reasonably expect that some parts of the country would be more prosperous than others. But you would also reasonably expect that there would be a gradual shading off from the best to the moderately good, to the only fair, to the poor, to the bad, to the very bad. But this is not so at all. The worst of the four good divisions is the Midlands. The best of the four bad divisions is the north-west. But the abnormal unemployment in the north-western division is more than twice as large as in the Midlands. You have four good divisions, then a big bump, then four bad divisions.

The four good divisions and the four bad divisions are each of them almost exactly half the whole country—that is, they each have half of the total workers, employed and unemployed together. But in one half there are only 320,000 persons abnormally unemployed; in the other half there are 1,130,000. Abnormal unemployment in one half of the country is more than three and a half times as bad as in the other. Let me put it as graphically as I can. Take a map of Great Britain. Put your pencil on the town of Chester. Now draw a line due east from Chester until it hits the North Sea just north of the Wash. Then draw another line

from Chester due south until it hits the Bristol
Channel just east of Newport, Monmouthshire.

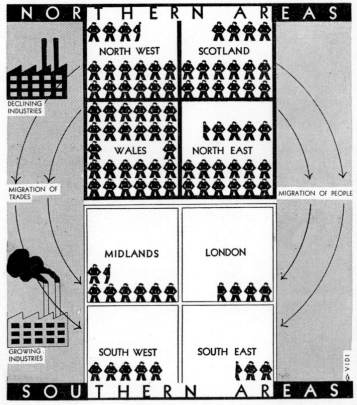

Each figure represents 1 per cent of abnormal unemployment

PROSPEROUS AND DEPRESSED AREAS

To the south and east of that boundary you have
a country which has its bad spots, but is, on the

whole, remarkably prosperous—perhaps the most prosperous country there is in the world. North and west of the boundary you have another country which is one of the most depressed in the world. We are all of us, of course, familiar with the fact that there are depressed areas in the north, in Scotland and in Wales. But I think very few people realise how completely the country is divided into Two Nations, one rich and one poor, one depressed and one on the verge of prosperity. People who live in the prosperous south simply have no conception of the meaning of depression as it has been inflicted on the depressed nation of Outer Britain.

This inequality of unemployment is much the most striking thing that is to be discovered from the unemployment statistics. It is, so far as I know, a circumstance that is peculiar to Great Britain and is not repeated in any of the other great industrial countries. Moreover, I suggest that there is one very important lesson to be learned from it. If unemployment is thus concentrated in one half of the country, we must look for the cause of unemployment in something which has affected that one half much more than the other. It is no good suggesting as the cause of unemployment something that works equally all over the country— such an explanation simply would not fit the facts. It is no good, that is to say, maintaining that the breakdown of the Capitalist system is the cause. Why should it have broken down three times worse in one part of the country than in another? Nor can it be due in the main to any defect of the money system, which would have affected Oxford as much as Oldham. Both these things, faulty Capitalism and faulty money, may have played some part, but the facts demonstrate that neither of them can have been the major cause.

This strange and striking contrast can be carried still further. We have now had just about three years of fairly steady recovery. The south at the worst period of the depression had 12 per cent of abnormal unemployment. The north has 18 per cent even now after three years of recovery. Let me translate those figures into words. The south (meaning by the south the four good divisions of London, the south-east, the south-west and the Midlands), even in the darkest days of 1932, had only half as much abnormal unemployment as the north. After three years of recovery, unemployment in the north is still half as large again as it was in the south at the very bottom of the depression. Recovery has removed more than half the abnormal unemployment in the south, but only just over a quarter in the north. I could go on with contrasts of this sort for a long time. Is it any wonder that the people who live in this depressed half of the country complain that their plight is not fully understood in the south? In Great Britain more than in most countries of the world, public opinion is formed and given expression in the capital city. If London happened to be in one of the bad divisions of the country, instead of being probably the most prosperous city in the world to-day, there would probably be a very different frame of mind towards this problem.

When there is such a striking disparity between the two halves of the country, it is only to be expected that there should be some migration from the depressed half to the prosperous half. In point of fact, there has been a very considerable migration. In July 1934 there were half a million more jobs in the south than there had been in July 1927, and half a million less in the north. The south has been gaining on the north at the rate of 70,000 persons a year or nearly 1400 a week. Moreover, as might be expected, it is the most prosperous divisions which have gained most and the least prosperous that have lost most. But all the four "good" divisions have gained workers, and all the four "bad" divisions have lost. It does not, of course, follow that migration has been as large as that. An increase of one in the number of jobs in London may mean a London boy getting his first job after leaving school rather than a former Welsh miner starting life again as a bricklayer's labourer in London. But though we cannot say exactly how large the migration has been, it has undoubtedly been very large.

There has also, of course, been a considerable migration from industry to industry. There are accurate figures bearing upon that and I commented on some of them in Chapter 2. Let us take the four industries which have lost the greatest proportion of their workers and compare them with the four industries which have gained most recruits. The four losers are coal-mining, iron and steel, shipbuilding and marine engineering—every one of them centred in the North of England, Scotland and Wales. The four greatest gainers are electrical apparatus, public works contracting, cement and artificial silk—all but one of them concentrated in the South of England. There are consequently two questions which we must ask ourselves. First, why are some industries gaining at the expense of others? And second, why are the industries that are growing concentrated in the South of England?

The reason why some industries decline and others expand is sufficiently obvious. Most of the losing industries are those whose foreign market has shrunk. But some of them are shrinking for purely internal reasons. Dressmaking, for example, shows one of the largest declines, and it is due entirely to the fact that women can now buy excellent mass-produced dresses very much more cheaply.

On the other hand, the industries that are growing
are a more mixed lot. Some of them are due to
new inventions. There are, for example, the
electrical and chemical industries, both of which
have been assisted by inventions. Artificial silk
falls into the same category. Then there is a group
of industries connected with road transport, which
has been developing very fast—the actual manufacture of motor vehicles, the supply of petrol,
oil and rubber tyres, the driving of motor vehicles,
the public works contracting industry which
builds the roads—all these show increases. Then
there is a group of industries which are growing
because people are more and more tending to pay
other people to do things they used to do at home.
Laundries, hotels, the manufactured food industries—these again show increases. One of the
most interesting cases is that of shopkeeping. For
the past two decades there has been a great increase
in the number of people employed in shops and
similar forms of trade. This is a matter to which
I shall have to return in some detail later on. And
finally, there are some industries which are expanding because the mass of the people have more
leisure, chief of them being entertainment and
sport and printing. Now this, I think you will
agree, is a very varied catalogue. I have distinguished five groups, which are worth recapitulat-
ing: (1) technical inventions; (2) the special case

of road transport; (3) what I call the "mechanical housewife" industries—that is, laundries, hotels, restaurants, etc.; (4) wholesale and retail shop-keeping; and (5) the leisure trades. These five groups between them include virtually all the industries that are growing.

But we haven't really got very far yet in explaining why they have all—or nearly all—chosen to expand in the south and not in the north. A number of reasons have been given from time to time for this preference for the south. It is said, for example, that the burden of rates is much heavier in the north. It is quite true that the average level of rates is higher in the north, in Scotland and in Wales. But, especially since industry was very largely de-rated six or seven years ago, the burden of rates on industry is very low. Another reason that is sometimes given is that wages are lower in the south—but the difference, if there is any, must be very small. It is also said that the Trade Unions are stronger in the north and that employers come south to avoid them—but there again I doubt if there is really very much truth in the suggestion. All these factors may play their small parts, but I cannot believe that, even in combination, they make a great deal of difference.

In some cases, of course, it is a matter of pure historical accident. Take the motor-car industry, for example. It grew quite naturally out of the bicycle industry. And the bicycle industry, when it started forty-five years ago, inevitably settled in the Birmingham - Coventry - Wolverhampton district, because that district had always concentrated on the small metal trades and light engineering and it had the right sort of craftsmen handy. Thus, it was largely an accident that the motor-car industry settled where it did. But accidents cannot explain the whole business. The concentration of new industries in the south and their avoidance of the north is too remarkable to be explained by coincidence.

I think that this drift of industry can be at least partly explained by examining the nature of the new industries. Notice, for example, the following facts. First, there has been a very steady change over from industry (that is, making things) to trade. Trade, ever since the dawn of history, has tended to concentrate in trading centres, and London is incomparably the greatest trading centre in Great Britain, or even in the whole world. Apart from this shift from industry to trade, there have been large changes inside industry. The old heavy industries—that is, industries dealing with heavy materials in bulk—have declined and the light industries have been growing. Light industries do not need to be located on top of their raw materials or at the ports. The north has great

advantages for the heavy industries, but not for
the light industries, which are free to choose, and
frequently choose the south. Or again, take another
change. The new industries are almost all industries which sell direct to the consumer. The
motor-car industry, for example, though it manufactures cars by mass production, has to sell them
one by one. The old staple industries of pre-war
Britain, coal and cotton and steel, used to sell their
goods by the shipload. It didn't matter where they
were, so long as they could get easily and cheaply
to the sea. But the new industries must either be
near their customers or in a place where they can
reach their customers easily. London fills the bill
in both ways. A third of all the possible customers
in Great Britain live in London and the ten
counties surrounding it. They buy very nearly
half the new cars sold every year. So that even if
the motor-car industry had not happened to be
born comparatively near London, it would almost
inevitably have had to move there. And in other
cases when it is a question of distributing goods in
small quantities all over the country, like biscuits,
or artificial silk stockings or wireless sets, there are
great advantages in being in or near London,
because all the roads and railways in the country
lead to London. And in the case of printing,
whether of books or newspapers or magazines, it
is easy to see why the London district has an

insuperable advantage over other places. In fact, printing has become concentrated in London to such an extent that it is now the largest of all London's industries.

So, you see, there are several very strong reasons for the drift of industry to the south. Of course, they don't apply in every case. Some of the new industries have to be spread pretty evenly over the country from their very nature. For example, laundries cannot be concentrated in London, and the great development of motor buses has occurred in every part of the country. The same could be said of cinemas. But even then there will tend to be rather more development in the prosperous south, where people have more money to spend on laundries, on bus rides and on going to the pictures. There is a cumulative element in the whole business. Because one set of industries goes to the south it becomes profitable for another set of industries to follow them.

But when all is said and done, no explanation and no set of explanations is sufficient to explain a matter which is and will probably remain a mystery. Nevertheless, I have tried to show that there are some real reasons for the move to the south, because the realisation of that fact sheds some light on the next question. That is—what should we do about it? If it were mere chance, mere caprice, mere coincidence that all these industries were settling in the south and ignoring the north, there would be an unanswerable case for the Government interfering to reverse the trend. For example, I suspect that in some cases the deciding reason in favour of starting a factory just outside London has been the desire of the managing director—or perhaps his wife—to live in the West End of London. Now if this were the only reason, it is obviously a selfish reason, and if that factory were made to go up to County Durham or to the Rhondda Valley instead, the sacrifice made by the managing director would be more than compensated by the gain to the hopeless unemployed of the north or of South Wales.

But if, on the other hand, there is any real reason why the industry would be less efficient if it were in Wales or Scotland than in London, we ought surely to be more careful in compelling it to go to the distressed areas. If you want a specific case, take this one which received considerable prominence a few months ago. A large industrial firm which has always had its works in South Wales, announced that it would move the greater part of its business to Lincolnshire. South Wales is bitterly depressed, Lincolnshire at least relatively prosperous. But the change would mean more unemployment in depressed South Wales, more jobs in prosperous Lincolnshire. The company was not moving out of sheer contrariness or from dislike of South Wales. It was moving because it could produce more cheaply in Lincolnshire than in South Wales. If it stayed in South Wales it could not compete in the world market; if it moved to Lincolnshire, it could. Now, in that particular case, in those particular circumstances, would you have prevented that company from leaving South Wales? Or, transferring the question to the larger canvas, would you force new industries to settle in the depressed areas? If not all, which industries would you compel? And how would you distinguish between them?

I shall not stop to answer these questions, but shall leave them to you. I want to look very briefly at another aspect of the movement of population within this country—the movement from the country to the town. That movement has, of course, been going on for at least a century. But in the last fifteen years it has taken a different form. People are no longer crowding into the centre of the cities. Indeed, the central districts are losing population. The County of London, for example, actually fell in population by nearly ninety thousand people between the Census of 1921 and the Census of 1931, and the same sort of thing has been going on in other large cities. It is the districts surrounding the large cities which have grown so enormously, those vast suburban growths which stretch for so many miles in every direction

round our large cities. One result of this is that
the official figures have got thoroughly muddled.
Many of these suburban districts are still officially
classed as rural. You will find it solemnly recorded,
for example, that the rural population of Middlesex increased two and a half times over between
1921 and 1931. But nobody believes that this was
an influx of farmers, or even of market gardeners.
It was an influx of people working in the city and
living in the suburbs. The movement of population
has overrun all city boundaries. London is an excellent example. In the Middle Ages, London was
contained in the square mile between the Temple
and the Tower. Fifty years ago the County of
London was carved out of the neighbouring
counties of Middlesex, Essex, Kent and Surrey.
The County of London extends on the average
about five miles from St. Paul's. This was London
fifty years ago, and this is the London of the
London County Council even to-day. But London
soon overflowed those boundaries and the expression "Greater London" came to be used.
Greater London extends about fifteen miles from
Charing Cross. But since the war London has
spread even further than that and, in 1932 when
Parliament set up the London Passenger Transport Board, it defined London as an area extending
about thirty miles from the centre. Even that area
is too small in some respects.

This great suburban growth has been made possible by a number of technical inventions. First and foremost, of course, the petrol engine. But electricity, the telephone, and the cinema have also played their parts. Indeed, these inventions have done more than merely make sprawling suburbs possible. They have made it possible for industry to move out into the countryside. It is no longer necessary for an industry to be close to coal, because power is everywhere available in the form of electricity. Communications between one town and another are now better than they were between different districts in the same town fifty years ago. There are people who say that the whole justification for the huge city is disappearing, that the great cities will slowly give place to small towns. These people argue that the town with a population of fifty thousand is the ideal place to live—large enough to give the urban amenities and yet small enough for the country to be within reach without effort or expense.

This view is perhaps exaggerated. But I do think that it is true that there will be a tendency for some industries to settle in small towns rather than in the large cities and that the growth of the suburbs is a sign of the tendencies that are afoot. We may be at the beginning of a movement of "Back to the Countryside".

But "Back to the Countryside" does not mean

F

"Back to the Land". For many decades there has been a slow drift of workers away from agriculture. We now have fewest people on the land, proportionately to our total population, of any large country in the world. The proportion is small because we buy so much of our food from abroad. And it is falling because agricultural science is constantly discovering means of growing more food with less labour. Some people say that it is a disgrace that so few people are earning their living on the land—a disgrace which must be removed at once by a thorough-going policy of settling men on the land. Other people say that, on the contrary, it is the normal and natural tendency for the proportion of all workers on the land to fall. Civilisation, they say, did not begin until workers started to leave agriculture, and the more developed a country is the fewer people it will have on the land. In my experience this is not a quarrel that can be settled by reason or by facts. It is a matter of emotion—it all depends how you happen to feel about it.

5. SUPPLYING THE CONSUMER

HITHERTO we have been speaking about the ways and means of making goods and performing services—about the people who make the goods or perform the services, the industries in which they work and the places in which they do their work. We have, in fact, been almost entirely concerned with *work* and have had very little to say about the purpose of work. We must now begin to remedy that defect. What is the purpose of this whole vast complicated economic machine, driven by the power of human work? Its purpose is to serve the ordinary citizen of the nation. The modern economic mechanism is so complicated that it is often difficult to perceive the ultimate purpose of some of its intricate parts. The man who rolls steel rails, or mines iron ore or mixes chemicals is often tempted to think that the ultimate purpose of his work is to produce steel rails or iron ore or sulphuric acid. But it is not so. These things in themselves are useless. They are worth making, worth spending human effort to procure, only because they play some tiny part in increasing the supply of goods and services available to the ordinary consumer. Modern industry moves on devious routes, it produces in the mass, it has specialised and sub-specialised its functions until the complications of the system have become too great for any one man to understand. But industry comes back in the end to the individual consumer. All the complication, all the effort, has one purpose only—to increase the welfare of the individual consumer, to meet more of his needs, to supply more of his wishes and desires.

The governing philosophy in many of the states of continental Europe would deny this statement. They maintain that the purpose and end of industry and trade is not to enrich the individual or make his life pleasanter, but to strengthen the State, to increase its prestige, to place it above its enemies. They say that the individual must be prepared to make any sacrifice, whether the economic sacrifice of poverty or even the physical sacrifice of his life, if thereby the State is glorified. That is not the British conception. It is true that we devote some of our resources to things which do nobody any good, which are not intended to do anybody any good—such as guns and poisonous gas, tanks and bombers and battleships. But we regard them as a painful necessity, as an exception to the main purpose of our economic system, as an insurance policy to ensure that the bulk of our endeavours may be peacefully devoted to serving the interests of the individual consumer. The wealth or happiness of the individual consumer is the only justifiable economic end of any work or of any economic system.

In this chapter, therefore, I am going to discuss one or two things concerned with the consumer. First of all I am going to ask, and attempt to answer, the question, "Who is the consumer?" Then I shall have something to say about the organisation by which the goods produced in such profusion by industry are put into his hands.

Who is the consumer? In one sense the answer is obvious. We, all of us, are the consumer, the whole 45 millions of us in the country, men, women and children, old and young, rich and poor. Every one of us is a consumer, and in our mass we make up that powerful anonymous creature, the consumer. But an answer of this sort doesn't really carry us very much further. It is no good saying that there are 45 million consumers, unless you know what sort of people they are and what their wants are likely to be. In particular, we want to know how those 45 millions are changing. Our first task must therefore be to see what we can discover about the population of this country.

It so happens that the present is a particularly interesting time to enquire into the facts of population. For something like two or three centuries the population of this country has been steadily on the increase. This increase has been going on for so

long that most of us instinctively regard it as a
natural tendency. But it was not always so. All
through the Middle Ages the population of
England was stationary. Indeed, there were times,
such as the Black Death in the fourteenth century,
when the population declined. The Merrie England of Queen Elizabeth had only something like
an eighth or a tenth of the population of England
to-day. The rapid increase did not begin until
nearly the end of the eighteenth century. The first
census was taken in 1801 and it showed a population of Great Britain of only just over 10 million
people—less than a quarter of what it is now. At
the time of Waterloo there were only just about
as many people in the whole of Great Britain as
there are now in London. The population doubled
in Queen Victoria's reign alone.

You must not, therefore, think of the population having increased steadily since the dawn of
history. You must think of a population remaining
steady, or perhaps very slowly increasing, for
century after century. Then suddenly, at the time
of the Industrial Revolution, the population starts
multiplying with enormous speed. The period of
rapidly increasing population has lasted only about
150 years, only a tiny fraction of our history. Not
only *has* it lasted only 150 years, it *will last* only
150 years. For it has already come to an end.
Throughout the Victorian Age the population was

increasing by 300,000 every year. For ten years after the beginning of the war, the average increase was over 200,000 a year. But by 1933 it had dropped below 100,000, and there is now hardly any increase at all.

The rising trend of population is thus coming to an end. This is due entirely to a fall in the birth-rate, which has been falling for many years. It is due to fewer births and not to any increase in the death-rate. Indeed, if medical science had not succeeded in *lowering* the death-rate, the fall in the population would have come much earlier. The record number of births was in the year 1920, but that was the wholly exceptional result of the end of the war. If there had been no war and no consequent separation of families, many of these 1920 children would have been born in 1916, 1917, 1918 and 1919. Apart from the exceptional year 1920, the highest number of births was recorded as long ago as 1903. Ever since then births have been falling off. Now, with a population of 45 millions in Great Britain, we have only as many births each year as we had in the 'fifties, with less than half our present population.

We are thus at the very peak of our national population. Many of the experts on the subject maintain that it may quite probably reach the top in 1936, and that is why a number of eminent statisticians have asked the Government for a special census in 1936, so that we may have an accurate figure for the highest population this island is ever likely to contain.

What is likely to happen after 1936? The population will remain very steady at about the same figure for quite a long time. By the time the next regular census is taken in 1941 the population will probably be larger than in 1931, though slightly less than in 1936. Even in 1951 there will not be much change. But after that the population will begin to fall.

Now I can imagine you asking, how do I know that? How can I predict that with such assurance? How can anyone say how many people there will be in the future, when the figure depends upon babies not born and deaths still to happen? In point of fact, it is possible to predict future population much more closely than you might think. I believe this is a subject which is of very general interest, so perhaps you will forgive me if I try to explain very briefly how it is that we know what is going to happen to population in the future.

The number of births depends upon two things. First, it depends upon the number of women who are of the right age to have children—let us say, very roughly, between the ages of twenty and forty. And secondly, it depends upon the number of children that each woman has on the average. Now we already know how many mothers or

AGE 0 - 14 YEARS | AGE 15 - 59 YEARS | 60 YEARS AND OVER

1935

1945

1955

1965

1975

EACH FIGURE REPRESENTS APPROX.
3% IN EACH YEAR STATED

VIDI

CHANGE IN AGE OF POPULATION

potential mothers there will be a generation hence, because they are already born. If the average age of a mother is thirty years, we can say that we know already how many mothers there will be in 1965, and we can guess pretty closely even further ahead than that.

We do not know with equal certainty how many babies these mothers will have thirty years hence. The number of babies to every mother is a figure which changes only very slowly; it never moves in jerks. For many decades now it has been slowly falling. Let us suppose that it goes on falling for the next thirty years just as it has been falling for the past sixty years. If we suppose that, we can predict how many babies each the mothers of 1965 will have. And that will give us the total number of births thirty years hence. And when we know how many baby girls will be born in 1965, we shall know how many mothers there will be in 1995 and so on. Naturally, the further we go into the future, the more difficult it becomes to calculate accurately. But for the next thirty or forty years, we can be reasonably sure of our facts. And the facts foretell, first, that the population will not increase any more, and that later on it will begin slowly to decline.

Now the size of the population does not, perhaps, matter quite as much as people sometimes think. But something else, which very rarely gets mentioned, matters very much, and that is the proportions in which the total population is divided into old and young. When the population is increasing, there is always a high proportion of young people, because each generation as it comes along is larger than the one before. But when the population ceases to increase, the proportion of young people begins to fall. And when the population starts to fall, each new generation is smaller than the one before, so that there comes to be a very large proportion of elderly people. Let me put it as graphically as I can. The babies who were born round about the year 1903 were more numerous than in any period before or since (apart from the exceptional year 1920). Now that they are round about thirty years old, they are still the largest generation. And in 1963, when they are sixty years old, they will still be proportionately the largest generation of their time. Some of the people who specialise in this sort of thing have worked out exactly what this means. At present 23 people out of every hundred are less than fifteen years old. In 1965, there will only be 10 children out of every hundred—less than half as many as now. At present 12½ people out of a hundred are over sixty. In 1965 the figure will be 23½—almost double as many old people. In this next thirty years the *total* of the population will not change very much—it may be perhaps 5 or 6 millions lower. So the most striking change in the next thirty years will be, not a rapid fall in the total population, but this very remarkable change in the age of the population, a doubling of the old and a halving of the young.

Now I fully expect that as soon as the population is seen to be falling, there will be a large popular outcry and societies will be founded to start propaganda in favour of large families. But however fierce the propaganda it will not succeed in preventing the population from falling. The birthrate is falling now, partly because mothers have fewer children and partly because there are fewer mothers. Now do what we like, we can't alter the number of mothers—they are already in existence. We know already how many mothers there will be between now and 1965. We can try to persuade mothers to have more children. But, in the first place, it is very doubtful whether we should succeed: no government has ever yet succeeded in deliberately increasing the birth-rate for more than a year or two. And even if we did succeed in getting more children born, they would not be able in their turn to have children for thirty years.

The truth is that a declining population has been inevitable for a very long time. There are fewer mothers to-day because in 1903 the number of babies born in a year started to fall. And the number of births started to fall in 1903 because, thirty years earlier, the birth-rate had started to fall. And the birth-rate started to fall in the 'seventies because even earlier still mothers had started to have smaller families. The whole thing has taken nearly a hundred years to work itself out. And even if we succeeded in reversing the trend now, it might be another hundred years before the population started to increase again. These great movements in population move slowly, but once started they are almost beyond the power of Man to influence.

But we must not forget that we got on to the subject of population by setting out to find the consumer. What economic effect will these changes in population have? We do not know from experience what the effects of a falling total population will be because there has been no modern industrial State which has ever experienced a rapid fall. But we need not trouble ourselves unduly with that, for it will be at least thirty years before the total population starts to fall at all rapidly. What we must trouble ourselves about, since it is already right on top of us, is the change in the age of the population. Now, broadly speaking, the people of working age, between fifteen and sixty-five, support the rest of the population. At present every two men and women of working age have, on the average, to support one dependant between them, either a child below fifteen or an elderly person over sixty-five. This proportion will not alter very much, at least for thirty years. What will alter is this. Out of every three dependants, two are now children and one an elderly person. In 1965, one will be a child and two old people.

Some of the effects of this are obvious. There will be a slump in the perambulator trade and a boom in bath-chairs. The firms now making patent baby-foods will have to turn to tonics for the elderly. The baby shops will find their business cut in half, while those catering for the elderly will do a roaring trade. But the effects go deeper than that. For one thing education will be a much simpler business. With only half as many children to educate, it will be possible to make many of the educational advances which are too expensive now. In 1965 we may be able to give universal free education up to the age of eighteen with free meals thrown in for very little more money than primary education costs to-day.

But if the children's problems will be made easier of solution, the problems of old age will be much more difficult to solve. Just imagine what the position will be when there are twice as many old men and women as there are now. It is difficult enough now for any old person to support himself. We know from the unemployment figures, for example, that unemployment among men over sixty is very much more severe than among young men. In thirty years' time, unless we do something about it now, there will be a very serious problem of unemployment among old people. Do not think that I am imagining bogeys. I cannot tell you to within a thousand or a hundred thousand just how many old people there will be in 1965. But that there will be many more than there are now is almost as certain as that the sun will rise to-morrow. It is not very often that we are able to see problems approaching from a long way off. In the rare exceptional case like this there is all the more reason for taking precautions in good time.

This matter of population provides almost endless themes for discusion. But we must get back to our friend the consumer. We must leave the fascinating population problem and pick up the second question we are going to discuss in this chapter.

We have seen who the consumer is and who he is likely to be. Later I shall have something to say about the changes that are going on in his tastes and desires. For the remainder of the present chapter I want to discuss the link between the consumer and the industrial system. On the one hand you have this vast complicated system, busily turning out goods and services. On the other hand you have the consumer. The two meet in the shop. It is to the shop I now turn.

Unfortunately, in turning to the question of shops, we are turning to a subject on which there is very little information to be had. In almost every other industry we have at least a certain basis of fact to build upon. But for the industry of distribution there is almost nothing. The industry is scattered in small units up and down the country and it would admittedly be difficult to collect accurate information. But the difficulties are probably no greater than in the case of agriculture, where we have quite a lot of information collected every year. So far as productive industry is concerned—that is, the industries which *make* things —the Government takes a special census of production every few years. There was one in 1924 and another in 1930 and still another has been taken in 1935. In these censuses of production, every firm has to give information about the number of people it employs, the value of the products it turns out, and so forth and so on, and the results are invaluable to anyone who wants to know what is going on in British industry. It has been suggested recently that there should be a similar census of distribution, which would for the first time give us some actual hard facts about the shop industry. But until this is done we are left with very little to go on. Even the unemployment figures are of very little use, for so very many of the people who work in shops are their own masters and consequently not insured against un-employment. So in what I have to say about shops, I can be far less certain of my facts than on most of the subjects which are touched upon in this book.

But I think there are two large facts which can be stated about the distributive trades. The first is that there has been a very large increase in recent years in the number of people who earn their living by selling things. This is the one hard fact that we know for certain, because the census of population, which takes place every ten years, gives us figures of the trades that people belong to. Between 1921 and 1931 the number of people occupied in wholesale and retail trade increased from just over 2 millions to very nearly $2\frac{2}{3}$ millions, and it has undoubtedly continued to increase since 1931. That is really an enormous increase— an increase of one-third in ten years. It would be very hard to find any equally large industry—and distribution is a very large industry—which has increased since the war at anything like that rate. And there are very few that can show a similar increase even among the small industries.

The second outstanding thing we can say about distribution is not quite so certainly true, though there seems to be a lot of evidence to support it. This second fact is that the *cost* of distribution seems to be increasing, that a larger proportion of

G

the consumer's shilling appears to be going to the wholesale or retail trader, the middleman, and less to the actual producer of the goods. Here are two outstanding tendencies in the post-war shop which are well worth a brief discussion.

Let us take first the increase in the number of people working in shops, or in other forms of selling goods. Nearly every kind of shop shows a large increase. The number of people working in retail confectionery shops, for example, increased from 41,000 in 1921 to 55,000 in 1931, in groceries from 224,000 to 250,000. But there is one very interesting thing to observe. The shops which sell necessaries of life—which every family, including the poorest, must buy—showed smaller increases than the shops selling things which, in many families, are luxuries. Thus the number of grocers increased not much more than 10 per cent, but the number of people selling milk increased by 60 per cent, and the number of butchers by over 40 per cent. This suggests that one reason for the increase in shops was that people had more to spend, that the standard of living was rising.

What other reasons are there for the increase in the number of people earning their livings by selling goods? One reason can be found in the enormous amount of building that has been done since the war. All these new suburbs, these whole new towns, have had to be provided with shops.

Something like 6 or 7 million people are now living in houses that have been built since the war—the great majority of them in places where there never were houses before. All these people have needed shops, and the shops have been provided. But it is one of the most puzzling things about these new suburbs that the towns from which the people have come seem to be as crowded as ever. There have been more shops in the suburbs, but no fewer in the towns.

Another reason for the increase in the number of people working in shops is that there has been a considerable increase in the services which the shop performs for its customers. There were many thousands of shops in the old days which the proprietor ran without help. But nowadays he has to have one or two persons both to collect the orders and to deliver the goods. Delivery, in particular, is now done on a very much larger scale than it used to be, and even the small one-man shop cannot meet the competition of the large stores unless it can promise to deliver goods promptly. Then there is the question of credit accounts. These also have been on the increase and our one-man shop nowadays finds it has to get somebody in to look after the books. All these little extra services, which have been gradually, almost imperceptibly, on the increase, need extra people to perform them.

Still another reason is to be found in the depression of trade itself. Many thousands of people who have lost their jobs in industry have taken refuge in a small shop. One of the most striking things about the depressed areas is the number of small shops which have survived, and even increased their numbers.

And finally, an increasing number of people are engaged not so much in selling goods as in persuading other people to buy. The number of people occupied in advertising almost doubled between 1921 and 1931, while the number of canvassers increased more than six times over.

Let us then pass on to the second question. Why has the *cost* of distribution increased? But it really hardly counts as a separate question, because the biggest reason for the increased cost is to be found in the larger numbers of people in the industry. All these extra people have to be paid in one way or another and it is the consumer who pays. If an increasing proportion of the whole population is occupied in the distributive trades, it is inevitable that the cost of distribution should increase. When we have explained one fact we have simultaneously explained the other. If there are more shops in the suburbs, but no fewer in the towns, that can only mean that there are fewer customers on the average to each shop. And as the customers have to support the shopkeeper they will have to devote a larger slice of each shilling to that purpose. Extra workers delivering goods, more people in the book-keeping departments, more advertising agents, more canvassers—all these swell the numbers of people in the distributive trades, and the wages of each help to increase the cost of distribution.

Now this sort of thing is, in part at least, quite natural. I pointed out earlier in this book that as a nation gets more developed and as its standard of living rises it is a quite natural tendency for the proportion of people making goods to fall and for the proportion of people performing services to increase. Some people are accustomed to refer to the two groups as producers and parasites. But that attitude is, of course, entirely wrong. The shopkeeper is as much a producer of wealth as the man who actually bakes the bread or weaves the cloth. The only sensible question to ask is: Is he doing his job efficiently? Could it be done more efficiently in some other way? "More efficiently" always means—always must mean—with less expenditure of labour. And that sort of question is one that can be put equally to the shopkeeper and to the iron-founder, the canvasser and the cotton-weaver.

Is the distributive industry efficient? I wish I knew the answer. One thing at any rate is clear. Every year we are devoting a larger proportion of our national resources to distribution. Are we getting any equivalently increased return? If the number of shops were greatly reduced, if products were standardised, if there were less range of colours and varieties and sizes, if there were less advertising, if fewer goods were delivered and no credit extended—if all these things were done, I have no doubt that distribution would cost us a great deal less than it does to-day. Are all these extras, these trimmings, these etceteras, worth the extra price? The public will apparently pay for them, as is demonstrated by the remarkable expansion of shopkeeping since the war. But if the public *knew* that it was paying for them, would it still want them?

6. THE DISTRIBUTION OF THE NATIONAL INCOME

It was suggested in the first chapter of this book that you would find it helpful to think of every working member of the community contributing his goods or services to a great pool, from which we all draw. The system is co-operative in the sense that every one of us needs to draw from the pool some goods and services which others have contributed. Very few of us would even succeed in contributing anything without the help of others.

Hitherto we have been mainly concerned with the contributions to the pool. We have discussed who makes them, how and where. We have discussed the changes that are going on in the sorts of things that are contributed. In particular I have had a lot to say about the contributions made by the export industries and by the distributive trades.

Now I want to turn to the other side of the picture and have a look at some of the problems that arise in connection with the shares that we each draw out of the pool. Let us, therefore, suppose that the pool, the National Income, is there—an aggregate of goods and services available for the citizens of the country. Let us forget about all the problems connected with the way in which it gets there and the forms in which it gets there, and turn to the sharing-out of the pool. Let us forget the earning of income and turn to the spending.

Before we can start dividing up the National Income we must first have some idea of its size. Now the National Income really consists of all the goods and all the services available for the citizens of the nation in a year. The only really satisfactory way of stating its size would be to recite an endless catalogue—so many million loaves of bread, tons of meat, gallons of milk, suits of clothes, the use of houses, roads, cars, railways, the services of doctors, lawyers, police—as you can imagine, the list would have no end. So we have to take refuge in the very poor second best of expressing the value of all these things in money. This again is by no means an easy thing to do and whole books have been written about the different methods of doing it. I don't suppose that there are two experts in the country who would be in complete agreement about the correct method. But we hardly need to go into their quarrels now, and I mention them only so that you shall bear in mind that any figures I quote are approximate estimates.

Roughly speaking, the method is to add together the incomes of all the individuals in the

country. You will then have the value of all the
work done and of the other services rendered
in the country, and that is the value of all the
goods and services available for consumption.
At least it ought to be. But there is one very
large class of very hard workers who never get
paid a penny for their labour. I mean, of course,
the housewives of the country. Their work con-
tributes most emphatically to the wealth of the
nation, as the rest of us would discover very quickly
if they all struck work one morning. But because
they are not paid wages, we are unable to say just
how much in money their services are worth. Consequently, when we are valuing the National Income in money, we have to leave them out. This
is, of course, a very substantial drawback, and
when we say that the National Income is so-and-so
many million pounds, that must be taken to mean
"so-and-so many million pounds plus the invaluable services of the housewives of the nation".

There is another drawback to the method of
valuing the National Income in money. That is
that money changes its value from time to time.
For example, it has been estimated that the
National Income was about £2000 millions in
1911 and about £4000 millions in 1924. But that
does not mean that there were twice as many
goods and services available in 1924 as in 1911.
There probably were *some* more. We were all

probably, on the average, rather better off in 1924 than in 1911, but we were by no manner of means twice as well off. What had happened in the meantime was that the prices of all sorts of things had increased. You could get fewer loaves of bread or yards of cloth or miles of railway travel for a pound in 1924 than in 1911, and consequently £4000 millions in 1924 meant less than twice as much as £2000 millions in 1911. Exactly how much less than twice as much we cannot, unfortunately, say.

But in spite of these defects, measuring the National Income in money is the only way there is, so we must make the best of it for lack of a better. The National Income in 1935 was, as in 1924, round about £4000 millions. That means that if the whole income of the country were divided up equally, every man, woman and child would have an income of about £87 a year, a shade more than 33s. a week. A family of three would have an income of about £5 a week, a family of five an income of just over £8 a week. You can easily apply that figure to your own family and see whether you are above or below the average.

But it is too early yet, of course, to speak with any confidence of the National Income in 1935. For purposes of comparison we must go back to the year 1931, when, since it was nearer the bottom of the depression, the National Income was about £3500 millions. In most of what follows I shall be talking about the year 1931, and you must remember that conditions may have changed since then. About two-fifths of the whole National Income is made up of wages and nearly a quarter of salaries. Wages and salaries together, therefore, amount to almost two-thirds of the National Income. Two-thirds of the National Income is the share going to those whose contribution is in the form of labour—labour of hand or of brain. The remaining third goes to those who contribute land and capital. These are the three so-called "factors of production"—land, labour and capital. Labour gets two-thirds, land gets a very small fraction, about a twentieth, and capital gets rather over a quarter. This division is a little misleading, since there are many thousands of very hard-working men who contribute a great deal of labour but, because they happen to be their own masters, their income is called profits and classified as the income of capital. But the distribution I have just given you is about as close as we can get—say 70 per cent labour, 25 per cent capital, 5 per cent land.

But these figures refer to 1931, which was the bottom of the depression. Profits always shrink fastest in a slump and increase fastest in a boom, and if we take a relatively prosperous year like 1929, we shall find the income of capital jumping up from 25 per cent to about 35 per cent, while the share of labour falls from 70 per cent to 60 per cent. So it is impossible to say just exactly what are the shares of labour and of capital; it depends on the year. Because labour only gets 60 per cent in a good year and 70 per cent in a bad year, does not mean that it is worse off in good years and better off in bad years. A small slice of a large cake may be larger than a big slice of a small cake. In point of fact the 70 per cent in 1931 was more than £100 millions *less* than the 60 per cent in 1929.

Why are there these changes in the share of the National Income which goes to labour—meaning by labour all those whose incomes consist of wages or salaries? The answer is that wage-rates in this country are relatively fixed and stable. They do, it is true, sometimes increase and they are sometimes lowered. But on the whole there are comparatively few changes in the standard rates of wages. This is not so in other countries. In both of the other two large industrial countries, for example, Germany and the United States, wage-rates have been cut and cut again in the years of depression. But, you may say, the total amount of money paid out in wages does not depend solely upon wage-rates. It depends also on the number of men there are in employment. That, of course, is true. But the variations in employment are not as large as you might think. An increase of unemployment from 1 million to 2 millions sounds very large. But when you think of it as a reduction in employment from 12 millions to 11 millions it does not sound so large. So when you have stable wage-rates and comparatively stable employment, the result is a pretty steady total of wages and salaries; not varying, that is, by more than 10 per cent either way. That at least has been our experience in recent years.

But, of course, the National Income as a whole varies much more than wages. Consequently, the larger part of the variations are concentrated on profits. In a bad year, profits are sometimes only half as much as in a good year. Indeed, in the United States, so severe was the slump that profits entirely disappeared at one period, the profits of those firms which had any being wiped out by the losses of the rest. Now from one point of view this is entirely right and proper. The people who earn their living by wages and salaries are, for the most part, comparatively poor. They are dependent on their earnings and few of them have savings of any size to fall back on. It seems right that they should have as steady an income as the economic system can give them. The people who get profits, on the other hand, are, on the whole, much better off. They have more savings put by and they are accordingly better fitted to meet the proverbial rainy day.

But unfortunately the matter is not quite as simple as that. For the people who get profits are also the people who manage industry, the people who say whether men shall be taken on or laid off. They are the people whose action decides the unemployment total. And when, in poor years, their profits are shrinking, it is only natural that the activity of industry should decline. The fact that profits vary so widely, shooting up in one year and shrinking in another, may be one of the chief reasons why unemployment falls and rises. This has led many people to argue that the way to get rid of booms and slumps, with all the unsettlement and misery they cause, is to prevent profits from jumping up and down so violently. And the way to do that, they say, is to make wage-rates move up and down much more freely than they do at present, up in good years, down in bad.

Now this is a real controversy. One school of thought says that when a slump comes, wages should be kept up by every possible means. In that way, they say, you will maintain the buying power of the great mass of the population. Britain, they say, has followed that policy during recent years, and as a result has come through this very difficult period much better than the other industrial nations. The opposing school of thought says that when a slump starts, wages should be reduced. Profits will then not fall very much and business men will not lay off as many of their workers as they otherwise might. On the other hand, when a boom comes, wages should be raised. Profits, they say, will not, under this system, be any larger on the average than under the other system. But they will vary less from year to year and consequently there will be fewer ups and downs in unemployment.

I have put those two opposing views somewhat crudely, but I hope clearly, before you. I do not think either of them is completely wrong. The ideal policy in a period of slump might involve some reduction of wage-rates. In point of fact, of course, no worker and no Trade Union can be asked to agree to a reduction of wages unless they know that they will get it back later on, and in this uncertain world such an assurance is very hard to come by. So reductions in wages are hardly practical politics. To discuss the matter further now would lead us very far afield. But in periods of bad trade it is possible that a small reduction in wage-rates would lead to a diminution of unemployment, and that insistence on the maintenance of wage-rates in full may mean an increase in unemployment. This is probably the case—nobody can be quite certain, but it seems reasonable to suppose that it is the case. If so, Labour has the choice between keeping wage-rates up or reducing unemployment to a minimum. Wages can be maintained at the cost of increased unemployment, or unemployment can be kept down at the cost of lower wages. I do not propose to say which is the right choice to make. But it is perhaps not always realised that there is a choice of evils, or that there is any connection between wage-rates and unemployment.

But I have been theorising and straying rather far from the actual ascertainable facts of Great Britain in 1935. Whatever may be the cause, and whether it is the best policy or not, the fact remains that the total income going to wage- and salary-earners in Great Britain has not recently varied very greatly from year to year. And when I say income, I mean the money that goes to the wage- and salary-earners, the pounds, shillings and pence. Although this has not varied very much, there has been one very significant change in the last six years. Owing to the great fall in prices, these pounds, shillings and pence will buy very much more in 1935 than they would in 1929. The reduction has been most marked in the case of food and clothes, but it has been taking place in almost every line. The money income of the British wage-earner has remained substantially unchanged. But his *real* income—the goods he can buy with his money income—has increased quite substantially. If you want it in figures, it has increased by one-eighth—he can buy nine goods for every eight he bought in 1929. In fact, I venture to make the statement that the wage-earner who has kept his job is better off now than he has ever been before. I expect that statement to be contradicted, but I believe nevertheless that it will stand up to any test. It is at least true that the consumption of all sorts of food and other necessaries has increased quite substantially in recent years.

But I am speaking only of those who have kept their jobs. They are the majority—the large majority—but we must not, after all, forget the 2 millions who are out of work. *Their* plight is undoubtedly worse than in 1929, if only because there are twice as many of them, and there is enough evidence of malnutrition and of poverty and of misery among them. In fact, a remarkable thing has been happening in recent years within the British working-class. On the one hand you have the majority, increasing their standard of living, thanks to cheap food and cheap clothes. On the other hand you have a growing minority of the destitute poor. The inequalities of income within the working-class, the contrast between the man with a job and the man without, are also greater to-day than they have been certainly in the last twenty years, and probably for even longer than that. You have the strange paradoxical contrast of growing poverty and growing prosperity side by side.

The evidence of the rising standard of living of the working-class must not be taken as an excuse

H

for complacency. My next point is very far indeed
from being a complacent one. I have just spoken
of an inequality of incomes within the working-
class. But any such inequality is of the most
trifling insignificance compared to the inequality
of incomes between rich and poor. The facts about
this inequality are truly amazing. The average
wage for a man is something like 65s. a week;
that can be taken as a fair average sample of wages
in British industry, and there must be million upon
million of men earning about that figure. Sixty-five
shillings a week is £169 a year. But there are
something like 500 people in this country who
have incomes of £169 a *day*. Let me take another
test. Let us call anybody with an income of more
than £2000 a year rich. Many people who have
that income think of themselves as poor, but to the
great mass of the people they seem to be very
decidedly rich. The law also apparently thinks
that riches start at £2000 a year, because it is
incomes over that figure that are liable to surtax.
Anyhow we will call them the rich. Anybody whose
income is less than £250 is liable to inclusion in
the National Health Insurance scheme, unless he
is specially exempted. Let us call these the poor.
Those between £250 and £2000 are the middle
classes. We can say roughly how many incomes
there are in these three classes. There are about
100,000 rich incomes, about 2,000,000 middle-

18,000,000   POOR (UNDER £250)

2,000,000   MIDDLE CLASS (£250 TO £2000)

100,000   RICH (OVER £2000)

VIDI

56%

28%

16%

THE APPROX. NUMBERS OF INCOMES

PERCENTAGE OF THE TOTAL NATIONAL INCOME

THE DISTRIBUTION OF INCOMES

class incomes and about 18,000,000 poor incomes. Putting it in another way, 90 per cent of the people are poor, 9½ per cent of the people are in the middle class and only ½ of 1 per cent are rich. But when we look, not at the number of people, but at the money they get, we get a very different picture. Sixteen per cent of the whole National Income goes to the rich, 28 per cent goes to the middle classes and only just over half to the poor. The rich and the middle classes together, who are one-tenth of the people, get almost half the income. The people with incomes of over £5000 a year—the very rich—are only one in a thousand of the people. But they get one pound in ten of the National Income. All these figures, I hasten to add, refer to incomes before taxes have been paid. The income tax, of course, takes a very large slice out of the larger incomes and the contrast would not be so startling if you compared incomes after the payment of taxes. But the contrast would still be very big, and the fact remains that our economic system allows people to get incomes as large as that, even if part of them is then taken away in taxes. Most people would willingly pay the income tax if only they could have the income.

Some of these large incomes come from salaries, fees and similar earnings. They can, if you like, be called the earnings of labour, though it is labour of a very specialised and expensive variety. But the great bulk of large incomes come from inherited property. There is no doubt that inheritance is the root of inequality. If you made it impossible for one man to inherit the property of another, you would at one stroke get rid of most of the inequality of wealth.

But we are running ahead a little too fast. Do we *want* to get rid of the present inequality of wealth? Many people would say "yes" unhesitatingly. But there are some arguments on the other side, arguments other than those used by the rich themselves, who might be thought to be biassed. What is the economic value of the rich? There are two arguments that can be made. In the first place, it is said that men must be allowed to make large incomes and pass on large estates to their children as a reward for taking the risks of business. If there were no large rewards, there would be nobody to take the risks of progress and the steady advance of the community would be hindered. The second argument is that the rich are necessary in order to do the community's saving: saving which is absolutely necessary for the community but which the poor cannot afford to accomplish. If these two arguments are correct, any attempt to reduce the inequality of wealth might have the effect of reducing the size of the whole National Income. The poor might get a larger slice, but it would be a larger slice of a much smaller cake. It is the fashion to deride these arguments, but they are by no means negligible. Notice carefully, however, what they amount to. They amount to a statement that the *present* incentive to enterprise is profits and that the *present* source of savings depends largely upon the incomes of the rich. It does not necessarily follow that no other incentive to enterprise and no other source of savings could be discovered.

There are, then, two opposing points of view. Our actual policy in Great Britain, however, is a compromise between the two. The State has not done anything very definite either for or against inequality. It is true that in the last twenty years very heavy taxes have been imposed both on incomes and on estates passing by death. It is true also that expensive social services have been founded. Later on, I shall be devoting a chapter to the finance of the Budget, and one of the questions I shall have to discuss is whether the poor have, on balance, gained or lost by the changes of the last twenty years. But if I may anticipate the conclusion of that future chapter, it is that the intervention of the State has done very much less to diminish the inequality of wealth than is usually supposed.

After all, there is one simple test. If the taxes which the rich are forced to pay are succeeding in reducing the inequality of wealth, you would expect to find a reduction in the number of large incomes. But, in point of fact, there is no such reduction. Just before the war there were 13,000 people with incomes of £5000 a year or more. Prices have risen since 1913, so that to buy the same things as you could buy with £5000 before the war, you might need about £8000 now. But in 1929 there were actually more people with incomes of £8000 than there were with incomes of £5000 in 1913. Or again, there are now nearly twice as many millionaires dying each year, on the average, as before the war. I do not think that anybody can look at these facts without coming to the conclusion that taxation has done very little to reduce the inequality of wealth. It has, perhaps, prevented it from getting any worse; but that seems to be about the limit of what it has done.

7. WHAT DO WE SPEND OUR MONEY ON?

WE must now turn to what is perhaps the most vital, and certainly not the least interesting, question of the whole subject. What do we spend our National Income on?

Before I begin to answer that question, let me just remind you of exactly what the National Income is. It is the total of goods and services available for the consumption of the individual citizens of the country. The test by which a thing can be included in, or excluded from, the National Income is this: can it be consumed by, or does it render a direct service to, some individual? Let me make that a little clearer by an example. Let us take a motor-car. Does it render a service to an individual? Yes, obviously; it enables him to get about from place to place and admire the countryside. The services of a motor-car are plainly part of the National Income. But now take a motor-lorry. Does it perform any service to an individual? Obviously, no. It takes its driver about from one town to another, but not because he wants to get about. He doesn't pay to be transported from London to Manchester—he is paid. Nobody gets any direct pleasure out of the motor-lorry. It helps, of course, to produce the National Income. But it is not itself part of the National Income. Similarly with all the machinery and the raw materials. They play essential parts in production. But nobody buys a stamping press or a cotton spindle or a railway engine or a ton of iron ore for his own use. When I come to list the things on which we spend our National Income, you must not, therefore, expect to find things of this sort. You will find only the sort of things that the families of the nation spend their incomes on. All the other things are paid for, of course. Wrapped up in the price of a loaf of bread there is payment for wheat, several kinds of transport, all sorts of machines, many varieties of labour. But all these things exist, not because they are good in themselves, but for the sole purpose of helping to make a loaf of bread, and it is only the loaf of bread that forms part of the National Income.

For the present, then, we can forget all about the complicated mechanism by which goods are produced and we need look only at the comparatively simple things that the complicated mechanism produces. We can regard the whole nation as one large family and we can enquire what this family spends its income on. And once again, I must add a caution. This is not a subject on which we can be precise. Any figures are estimates. Indeed, there are very few estimates to choose from. In what follows I am basing myself on some estimates made by Mr. A. E. Feavearyear, who has made a special study of this subject. Unfortunately, his latest figures refer to the year 1932, at the bottom of the depression, and the present state of affairs is different in several respects. But we must do our best with the material that is available.

I am going to divide the things on which we spend our income into seven classes. The first is food, with which I include drink and tobacco. The second is clothes. The third is houses; by which I mean more than just rent, but all those expenses that are necessary in the home (coal, gas, electricity, rates, miscellaneous household expenses such as soap and matches, and also wireless sets and wireless licences). The fourth item is taxes. Now many of the taxes are included in the price of other things. A large part of the price of beer, a small part of the price of tea and of other articles is tax. But these so-called indirect taxes cannot easily be separated from the articles on which they are levied. So, in my fourth item, I include only direct taxes—that is, those which have to be made by a special payment. Income Tax, of course, is the chief of them. The fifth item is sickness—doctor's fees, drugs, health insurance contributions and so forth. And, for the sake of convenience, unemployment insurance contributions are included here, although the sickness they represent is economic sickness rather than physical sickness. The sixth item is leisure and luxury. I include under this heading expenses on travel, including motor-cars, on entertainments, on sport, on books and newspapers, gramophone records, jewellery and a great variety of things that can be put under the all-embracing title of "fancy goods". And the last item is saving. Let me just repeat those seven headings: Food, Clothes, Houses, Taxes, Sickness, Leisure and Luxury, Saving.

Of those seven groups, we shall be concerned in this chapter in particular with three, so let us first get rid of the other four. Clothes is not a very large item; out of every £ of income, about 1s. 8d. was spent in 1932 on clothes. The clothing trades have already been discussed in two previous chapters and there is no reason to deal with them at length here. The most remarkable thing about our expenditure on clothes is that it has been falling quite rapidly. Ten years ago we spent something like 2s. 3d. out of every £ on clothes; now the figure cannot be more than about 1s. 6d. The explanation is to be found partly in the lower prices of textile raw materials, but mainly in the great reduction in prices which mass-production in the clothing trades has made possible. The greatest reductions have been in hosiery, in boots and shoes and in tailoring. There has been a silent

FOOD 8 s. 2 d.

CLOTHES 1 s. 8 d.

HOUSES 3 s. 2 d.

DIRECT TAXATION 2 s. 2 d.

SICKNESS 7 d.

LEISURE & LUXURY 3 s. 1 d.

SAVING 1 s. 2 d.

THE DISTRIBUTION OF EXPENDITURE

revolution in progress for many years past in the clothing trades, and it is a subject which would well repay special investigation.

Sickness is the smallest of the seven groups. Out of every £ in 1932 only about 7d. was spent in this way. But this also is rising, not because of any increase in sickness, but because of the larger sums that are being spent on the prevention of sickness. And you must also not forget that unemployment insurance contributions are included in this group and they have been increasing over the past decade.

The third group which I am going to dismiss briefly is taxation. Not because it is unimportant; on the contrary, it took 2s. 2d. out of every £ in 1932. And not because it is uninteresting, but because I am going to devote a whole chapter to taxation and the Budget. And similarly with the fourth group, saving. It is perhaps not always realised how vital saving is. A very large part of the National Income could not be earned at all if we had not inherited from our ancestors an enormous amount of capital equipment which assists us. Some of this capital equipment belongs to the community—roads, bridges, all sorts of public works and improvements, drainage systems, many of the water-works, public buildings and so forth. Other parts of this capital equipment belong to private persons or companies—railways, canals and all sorts of machinery. Without all this capital inheritance we should be little better off than the primitive savage. The community must go on saving in order, first, to keep this capital equipment up to date, and secondly to increase it. But this whole subject of saving is so very important that I am going to postpone it to a later chapter and say no more about it here.

That leaves me with three groups: food, houses and leisure and luxury. Let us start with food. Food, drink and tobacco is much the largest of the seven groups. In 1932 it took 8s. 2d. out of every £; more than twice as much as the next largest group. Together with clothes and houses it makes up the three prime essentials of existence. In 1932 we spent on these three 13s. out of every £: almost two-thirds of our whole income. And of this two-thirds, food is much more than half. There is no other item of expenditure which is anything like as important as food.

In view of this importance of food, let us examine it a little further. Food covers a variety of things, especially when drink and tobacco are included. I will not trouble you with any more figures, but the total of food can be split up further. Meat and fish is the largest food item, taking about a quarter of the total food expenditure. Poultry, eggs and dairy produce is the second. Fruit and vegetables comes third, liquor fourth and tobacco fifth. Such things as sugar, tea, coffee and cocoa, including sweets and chocolates, come next. And bread comes last on the list, taking only 6d. out of the £.

The changes that are going on in some of these items are rather interesting. The consumption of meat, for example, is on the whole increasing. But we are eating less beef, more mutton and a lot more bacon. There seems to be less taste for beef and more for mutton, though the change-over has undoubtedly been helped by the fact that mutton has been cheaper than beef. Another interesting change has been the great increase in the consumption of butter and a falling off of margarine and lard—that again is due to prices, as butter has fallen in price much more than margarine. We are consuming many more eggs than ten years ago, partly owing to the fall in prices, partly, apparently, to an increasing taste for eggs. The same applies to poultry. Milk has increased, but not nearly as much as condensed milk. Most of the other items have increased. One of the very few that shows no increase during the past ten years is bread, although the price of the loaf has fallen. Bread is rather a peculiar commodity, for it is about the only thing of which the poor consume more than the rich. Generally speaking, as a family's standard of living rises, as it can afford more meat and milk and eggs, it needs less bread.

So the fact that we are not eating any more bread is not necessarily a bad sign, it may be due to increasing prosperity. The money spent on liquor is falling quite rapidly. On the other hand, we are spending more money every year on tobacco.

Our total expenditure on food in a year comes to the colossal figure of something like £1,500,000,000 — a figure so large that it is almost impossible to grasp it. Now the most interesting thing about our food supply is that most of it comes from abroad. Some of it, of course, *has* to come from abroad. Such things as tea, coffee, cocoa, and many kinds of fruit cannot be grown in this country. Other things, like sugar, are much more easily grown abroad. But even of the things that can be grown and are grown at home, we buy more from foreigners than from British farmers. We grow at home only a quarter of our wheat, less than half of our meat, only just over half of our poultry and eggs, about a third of our fruit and vegetables. There are, in fact, only two foodstuffs of which we ourselves produce the bulk of our requirements. The first is milk, which cannot be imported because it would go sour before it could be sold. But even in the case of milk we buy much the largest part of our butter, cheese and condensed milk from abroad. The other case is potatoes, which are so heavy relatively to their value that it does not pay to transport them very far. Lumping foodstuffs all together, we produce at home two-fifths of our food. The other three-fifths has to be imported from abroad.

Now to a great many people this seems to be obviously a bad arrangement. They say that we should do whatever we can to increase the domestic production of food, so as not to be dependent on the outside world. In that way, they say, we should be relieved of the necessity of paying foreigners for our vital foodstuffs, and we should also be safe in time of war. There is also the argument that our population is at present "unbalanced", that we have too many people in industry and too few on the land. But that, as I said earlier, is not an argument that depends on reason or can be either proved or disproved by reason. There is no divinely appointed proportion in which the population should be divided between industry and agriculture, and whether you think our present proportion is right or wrong is purely a matter of the way you happen to feel. So I shall say no more about it.

But it is possible to apply the test of reason to the other arguments for increasing our domestic production of food. Let us look at one or two of them. First of all there is the argument that if we grew more of our own food we should not have to pay foreigners for it. Now that looks very reasonable at first sight. But let us give it a second look.

What does "paying foreigners" mean? It means, it can only mean, giving them British goods in payment. The only way in which nations can make, or receive, payment is by giving or receiving goods. If we grew more of our own food we should have to give the foreigner less of our own goods in exchange. That means there would be even less market for our exports. The export industries, which are already by far the most depressed in the country and responsible for at least half of the unemployment, would be still more depressed. After all, if we buy less from foreigners they will buy less from us. And our biggest trouble is that already they buy too little from us. It may be that we shall never be able to increase our exports again—though I think that is a pessimistic view. But surely we ought to think twice before doing anything that will make them even smaller than they are now. It is true that, if we grew more of our own food, we should have to pay less to foreigners. But, in our present circumstances, paying less to foreigners would be one of the biggest economic disasters that could possibly overwhelm us.

But that is not all. Why do we buy so much of our food from abroad? The answer is very simple —because foreign food is cheaper, much cheaper, than British food. The British farmer will grow more food, but only on condition that he gets more money for it. To grow a lot more food at home would mean increasing food prices. And that would mean reducing the standard of living of the people. I do not think it is possible to exaggerate the importance to us, socially and economically, of keeping food as cheap as is humanly possible. During the last few years, for example, it has enabled us actually to increase our consumption of food in spite of depression and unemployment. Our standard of living is based upon cheap food. We spend 8s. 2d. out of every £ on it. An increase of as little as one-tenth in its cost would wipe out the whole of the provision we make for sickness.

We can, if we want to, increase our home production of food. As the years go on and the standard of living rises, we shall doubtless eat more food, or at least better and more expensive food, and it might be a sound plan to ensure that this additional food to be consumed should be largely home-produced. But any attempt rapidly to reduce our present dependence on imported food can only mean a lower standard of living for everybody and increased unemployment in the depressed areas.

So much for the very large item of food. The next item I want to mention is houses. This item, you will remember, covers many things besides rent; it includes rates, gas, water, electricity and other household expenses. But rent is much the largest part of it and I am going to talk about rent alone. In 1932 we spent 3s. 2d. out of every £ on houses. That does not include the cost of the new houses that were built in that year, but merely the annual cost of our existing houses. Moreover, the amount is rising. Ten years ago it was only 2s. 7d. and by now it must be nearly 3s. 6d. It is rising, not because rents are rising—on the contrary they are falling slightly—but because we have many more houses than we used to have. One of the most interesting and surprising things about the last few years is that a large part of the money that has been saved on food and clothes is going into houses. In the last four years, for instance, we have built a million new houses. But we haven't pulled down anything like a million, or even a hundred thousand, old houses. The result is that we are spreading ourselves over a million more houses now than we were four years ago—and of course 11 million houses cost more to keep up than 10 million houses. So we are spending more of our income on houses. As a nation we spend about one-sixth of our National Income on houses— perhaps one-eighth on actual rent. But of course there are enormous differences between rich and poor. The rich with all their magnificent houses probably spend less than one-eighth of their income on rent. But many thousands of poor people spend more like one-third of their income on rent.

Now rent really includes two separate things. First of all, there is payment for the land the houses stand on, and secondly there is payment for the house itself. Now payment for the land is rather a peculiar thing, for land has no cost of production—you can't produce land. Land is worth only what people will pay for it. There is a school of thought which believes that nobody ought to be allowed to make land private property. God gave the land to the people, they say, and any private person who makes money out of it is a usurper. I am tempted to devote a few lines to discussing this idea, but space is limited and I will refrain from doing so. And in any case it is the less important part of rent. Unless you have a large garden or live in the most crowded and expensive part of a large city, payment for land is only a comparatively small part of the rent or of the mortgage interest you pay. Much the largest part of the value of the houses of the nation is the actual building cost of making them.

Of all the large items of expenditure, rent is the only one that gives real prospects of reduction. We are already getting our food as cheaply as we can; much of it we are actually getting at the moment below cost of production. Clothes have already been substantially reduced in price. Houses are the only one of the three primary necessaries of life left. And I am hopeful of some

reduction in rent in the future for this reason:
building is the only large productive industry
which has never had an Industrial Revolution.
Some of the things that go into houses—such as
window frames and sanitary appliances—are made
in large quantities in factories. But houses themselves are still made laboriously by hand, brick by
brick, as they were in ancient Egypt. I think it is
not impossible that we may be on the verge of a
great revolution in the technique of making
houses. It is possible that in future we shall make
houses in factories, just as motor-cars are made.
They will be standardised; but that does not mean
that all houses will be alike—any more than it
means that all motor-cars are alike. Three-quarters
of the houses that are built to-day are monotonously
similar, in any case. Now this may be a dream,
though I personally believe that we are very much
closer to it than you might think. But if it ever
should become a reality, we shall be able to reduce
very considerably our expenditure on houses.

What should we spend this extra money on?
Obviously on leisure and luxury; and that leads
me to the third group of items that I want to
discuss. Leisure and luxury took 3s. 1d. out of the
£ in 1932. The largest item was travel, in which I
include railway fares (railway fares for pleasure,
that is, not merely season-ticket travelling to and
from work), motor-cars and holidays. The next item

is entertainments and sport—theatres, cinemas, football, cricket, greyhound and horse racing, private amateur games, etc. Then there is expenditure on religion—if I may be forgiven for including that in leisure and luxury. Reading comes in here, too—newspapers, magazines, books —and also music and art. And then there are all the luxury trades that have not been included already under Food, Clothes and Houses—jewellery and cosmetics, for instance. Our expenditure on this very varied list of things is increasing. It was 2s. 7d. in the £ ten years ago, 3s. 1d. in the £ in 1932 and is probably higher than that now. In fact, expenditure on leisure and luxury naturally increases as the standard of living rises. As our incomes slowly increase, and as the cost of the primary necessaries of life falls, the margin is naturally spent in leisure and luxury.

Perhaps it would be more accurate to say leisure *or* luxury, because they are really alternatives. There are people who say that if we used to the full the potentialities of the machine we could have both leisure and luxury almost at once. But there is really no basis in fact for any such belief. It may be that if our organisation was improved we could produce many more goods than we do at present. If all the unemployed were set to work, for instance, we could produce 20 per cent more than we do at present. But any larger increase than that would mean an increase in the amount of goods which *each man* can produce, and there is really no evidence that, with our present knowledge, the average man's productivity can be increased very rapidly. It is, of course, increasing very slowly year by year, as new inventions and improved methods are applied; every year the average man seems to be able to turn out about 2 per cent more goods or services than the year before. But the only real scope for a *rapid* increase in the National Income is by utilising the idle labour represented by unemployment, and we have been trying, as a nation, for fifteen years to find some way of doing that. Even if we succeeded, and increased the National Income by one-fifth, we should still be a long way off *luxury* for *all*. And, at any time, now or in the future, whether we get rid of unemployment or not, it will always be true that the harder we work the more goods we shall have to consume. If we have more leisure we shall have less luxury.

Perhaps I can illustrate my point by a quotation from a broadcast talk by Mr. George Bernard Shaw. "If you had your choice," said Mr. Shaw, "would you work for eight hours a day and retire with a full pension at forty-five, or would you rather work four hours a day and keep on working until you are seventy?" Now that sounds like an interesting choice. But each of Mr. Shaw's alternatives mean less work and more leisure. Each of them, therefore, implies that many fewer goods and services are to be produced. If either of them were generally applied at present, it would mean starvation and utter destitution for the bulk of the people. On either of Mr. Shaw's alternatives, only half as much work would be done as at present. The only way of getting the same number of goods and services as at present with half the work is by doubling the amount that each man and woman can produce in an hour. And if anybody can tell me of a way in which we could all do twice as much work in an hour, I shall be very glad to hear of it. But it must apply to all of us; it must be a way by which the farmer can grow twice as much food, the bus conductor can take twice as many fares, the journalist can write twice as many articles, the shop assistant can serve twice as many customers, the housewife can cook twice as many meals and clean twice as many rooms. It is no good telling me that machines have enabled one man to make seven times more cars in a year now than twelve years ago. I know that; and I know that there have been similarly rapid increases in other mechanical industries. But the mechanical industries provide only a small fraction of the total National Income.

So I suggest that Mr. Bernard Shaw is really a hundred years too soon with his question. There has been a great deal of talk in the last few years

about the need for a forty-hour week, or even a
thirty-hour week, and many of the trade unions
are inclined to make a reduction of hours their
next objective rather than an increase of wages. It
is their business, of course, and not mine. But I
venture to ask whether we are really all so well off
now that there are no more goods and services we
want to consume. Shouldn't we make a little more
progress towards luxury before we begin to increase leisure? The productivity of the economic
mechanism is increasing at the rate of about 2 per
cent each year. That means that we can have
either 2 per cent more income each year or 2 per
cent more leisure. Or, if you like a bit of each, you
can have 1 per cent more income and 1 per cent
more leisure. But you *can't* have *both* a rapid increase in income *and* a rapid increase in leisure.
So I submit that the question Mr. Bernard Shaw
ought to have asked was this: "If you, you personally, were given the choice of *either* more
income *or* more leisure, but not both at once, which
would you choose?" I don't know the answer to
that, I can only answer for myself. But it is a
question which will have to be answered by
the people of this and every other country. And
the answer will be of supreme importance for the
future of the economic life of the world.

8. THE MONEY SYSTEM

I HAVE suggested earlier in this book that the easiest way of visualising the National Income is to think of all our labour, whatever its specialised variety, as contributing to a vast common national pool of goods and services. We all work to fill the pool, and we all live by drawing on the pool.

Now, of course, there is no such pool in existence, and never could be. In a very primitive community, where trades were few and wants were simple, it is possible to imagine such a great common market-place. The hunters of game would bring their catch to market and exchange it there for the grain grown by the tillers of the soil. The primitive tailor or hut-builder would barter his services for food. But in a modern community, with its immense complexity, any such simple process of barter is obviously impossible. Let me indicate only two difficulties out of many. Suppose that your job is playing the flute in a symphony orchestra and suppose that you want a new carpet for the dining-room. If we ran our system by barter, you would have to wait until some carpet-maker came along who was willing to give you a few square yards of best Axminster in return for a performance of the flute part in Beethoven's Ninth Symphony. In other words, it would be impossible to run our present system on those lines. Or consider another difficulty. How could you possibly decide how many minutes of flute-playing were worth one square yard of carpet —even if you did succeed in finding a carpet-maker with an eccentric taste in music? It would be impossible in such a crazy world to evolve any rational system of valuing different goods and services.

The great human invention which gets over these difficulties is Money. I have called it a great human invention, and so it is—perhaps one of the greatest of all Man's inventions. In the mechanical sphere, one of Man's fundamental discoveries was the wheel—a thing that exists nowhere, or hardly anywhere, in Nature. In the social sphere, the invention of money is equally fundamental. Both inventions are lost far back in the earliest ages of mankind, but each, in its own way, has been the basis on which all else depended. I think the analogy between the invention of money and the discovery of the wheel can be carried a little further. The wheel is essentially useless in itself. Nobody wants a wheel just for its own sake. The great utility of the wheel is that it makes it possible to do countless other things very much more easily. Just so with money; money is not wanted for itself. The economic system does not exist to make money; it exists to make food, clothing, houses, and all sorts of other consumable goods and services. Money is like the oil that lubricates a machine. It cannot make the machine, start it or stop it; its sole purpose is to help the machine to run more smoothly and more rapidly than it otherwise could. But if there is too much oil or too little or if the oil gets clogged or too watery, the machine will not run properly. So also money sometimes fails to perform its proper function.

The subject of money is one of the most complicated in the whole of economics. Not only complicated, it is also one of the most controversial. I cannot possibly do more in this chapter than take up one or two of the more interesting points connected with money and avoid as many of the controversies as possible.

The fundamental purpose of money is to assist the economic machine to work more smoothly. Let me return once more to my imaginary pool of goods and services to which we all contribute and from which we all draw. Now it is obvious common sense that the goods and services drawn out of the pool should be the same as those that are put into it. You can't draw out more than is put in; that is, you can't consume more than is produced. And if you try to take out less than is put in—if you try to consume less than is produced—there is obvious waste and you have the tragic paradox, from which we are now suffering, of Poverty in the midst of Plenty. The only practicable way of securing that consumption is equal to, or approximately equal to, production, is to value each individual's contribution to the pool, to give a ticket, or receipt, for the value of his contribution, and then let him take goods and services out of the pool to the value of the ticket he has been given. This, of course, is precisely what money does—or perhaps it would be more accurate to say, what money should do. A value is set upon the contributions of each one of us to the pool. The values sometimes seem very peculiar. It seems a little strange, to say the least, that the services of a man who daily risks his life in a coal-mine to get an essential raw material for industry should be given a very low value, while the services of a man who merely sits at home and allows his land to be built upon should be given a very high value. The system by which contributions to the great national pool of goods and services are valued may be unfair, but that is not the point at the moment; the point is that all our contributions are valued and we are given, on pay day, a receipt for that much value; and we can draw out of the pool only as many goods and services as we can get in exchange for that receipt. This is the fundamental purpose of money—to see that everybody gets out of the pool goods and services of the same value as those that he puts in. Money has other uses, which are important, but they are all supplementary to this fundamental function and it will be much less confusing if we forget about them for the present.

The technical name for this fundamental function of money is its function as a "medium of exchange". The important word there is "medium". Money is only an intermediary: nobody wants it for itself; nobody acquires money except for the purpose of sooner or later paying it away again. It is the intermediary that comes between the flute-player and the Axminster carpet. Now if money is to serve as a medium of exchange, what qualities must it have? That question is perhaps best answered by saying what qualities it need *not* have. To begin with, money need not be itself valuable. It is true that, for the greater part of the world's history, money has been made out of valuable substances such as gold and silver. It is also essential that nobody should be able to pick money off a tree; it is essential that there should be no more tickets in existence than there are goods and services in the pool. In other words, money must be limited in quantity, and throughout history the only possible way of ensuring that money was limited in quantity was to make it of some substance that was scarce and valuable, such as gold. But nowadays we have invented devices which make it very difficult and dangerous, if not quite impossible, for anybody to reproduce a pound note. Provided they are limited in number, pieces of paper serve just as well as pieces of gold.

The one essential quality of money is that it shall be acceptable. Anything which people treat as money—anything which they will give or accept in payment for goods and services of all kinds —is money. All sorts of things have been used as money in different places and periods. There are even some islands in the Pacific where the natives use huge stones as money. The stones are too heavy to move, but everybody knows who they belong to at any one time, and they are freely handed round—in a strictly metaphorical sense— in payment for transactions. If payment in stones is acceptable to the inhabitants of those islands, then stones are money in those islands. These particular islands belonged before the war to Germany, and the story is told that the German authorities had great difficulty in persuading the natives to provide the labour for road-making. Some bright person hit upon the idea of going round with a pot of paint and painting the German equivalent of the broad arrow on these stones, making them Government proprety. The natives then worked with a will to redeem their money, and when the road was built the Government went round and rubbed the broad arrow off.

That little story—which I have not, I assure you, invented on the spur of the moment, but which you will find in a most learned book on the anthropology of Polynesia—that story illustrates the fact that anything which is generally acceptable will serve as money. Perhaps I should spend just one minute more over this question of acceptability. If I were buying a suit of clothes from you, I might be able to persuade you to take payment in potatoes or woollen socks. I say I *might* be able to persuade you, but it isn't very likely, and in any case we shouldn't call that buying and selling, but merely barter or exchange, and I could hardly claim that my potatoes or my woollen socks were playing the part of money. But if I offered you a handful of silver coins or a few Bank of England notes, you would immediately accept them. In fact, coins or notes are accepted in payment for anything. Why are they accepted? Well, partly because the law says they *must* be accepted. If I owe you a debt and offer Bank of England notes in payment of it then you *must* accept: if you refuse to accept you cannot sue me for the debt. Notes are what is called legal tender. But it isn't only the law which makes money acceptable. Suppose I offered to pay for my suit of clothes by a cheque. If you knew me, and had reason to believe that I was not the sort of person who would draw worthless cheques, you would accept the cheque. Now I

shall be going on in a minute or two to say what a
cheque is. But there is one thing it is *not*. A cheque
is not money by law. There is no compulsion on
anybody to accept cheques in payment of anything.
Nevertheless they are acceptable, and something
like three-quarters of all the buying and selling
done in this country is done by cheques. There
are limits to the acceptability of cheques. You can't
buy railway tickets or postage stamps with them;
many shopkeepers do not like taking cheques
from perfect strangers. But nevertheless people *do*
buy things with cheques and they are sufficiently
acceptable to qualify as money. And, similarly, if
there were anything else which people were ready
to take in payment, not merely once or twice to
oblige a customer, but regularly and as a matter of
course, that thing would be money. If it became
the fashion to pay tram fares, or buy loaves of
bread, or pay the rent, with cowrie shells or beads
or banana skins, then cowrie shells and beads and
banana skins would be money.

There is nothing magical about money. The
community merely selects one commodity and
says, "This commodity shall serve as money; it
shall be acceptable in payment of debts; it shall
exchange freely for anything else in the world".
It is obvious common sense that money should be
something easily handled, unbreakable and unlikely to perish or go bad. But there are a great

many things that would serve as money and it is a point of comparatively little importance which of them we choose. Throughout most of the world's history money has been in the form of coins, which we still use for our smaller purchases. The bank-note is a comparatively recent invention —say three hundred years old—but it serves as money just as well, provided the proper precautions are taken to prevent forgery. And the cheque is a still more recent invention. It is only within the last hundred years that it has come to be the most important form of money, and even now it is comparatively little used outside the English-speaking countries.

It is about time that I tried to explain what a cheque is—and that will involve saying something about a bank. Cheques are the means by which something like three-quarters of the transactions in this country are settled. But they are nevertheless comparatively unfamiliar to the man in the street. But in the present-day economic system both cheques and banks play an essential part, and it is impossible to understand how the system works without paying some attention to finance.

It is very difficult to say, shortly and precisely, what a bank is. Parliament once found it necessary to define a bank in an Act of Parliament which was being passed—and the nearest that the combined wisdom and ingenuity of the Houses of Lords

and Commons could come to it was to say that a
bank is an institution that does a banking business.
So where Parliament failed I cannot hope to succeed. But we can say this much: a bank is an
institution that borrows from one set of people—
its depositors—and lends to another set of people.
But *what* does it borrow, and what does it lend?
Obviously, money. But you must not think that
money here means "coins and notes". It is only
comparatively rarely that you see anybody taking
actual coins and notes into a bank to deposit
them. The great bulk of the deposits are merely
slips of paper. And similarly with the borrowing.

Suppose I go to the bank and borrow £100.
I don't come out with 100 £1 notes. All that
happens is that the banker says, "You want to
borrow £100. All right, I will owe you £100, and
whenever you want it I promise to pay it to you."
What has happened is that we have exchanged
debts. I have put myself under the obligation to
pay £100 to the bank, and the bank has undertaken to pay £100 to me. A bank is, in fact, a
dealer in debts.

But there is this very important difference. If
I want to buy a motor-car for one hundred pounds
and offer my I O U in payment it will not be
accepted. But if I say to the car-dealer, "Look here,
instead of paying for that car in £1 notes, I will ask
Lloyds Bank to owe you that £100 instead of

owing it to me". Accordingly I write a cheque for
£100—that is to say, I write to the bank and say in
effect, "Dear Mr. Lloyd, you remember that £100
you undertook to owe me? Well, please owe it to
the car-dealer instead. With kind regards, yours
sincerely."

That is the real meaning of the words printed
and written on the face of a cheque. Now if
nobody had ever heard of this system before, and
I were now suggesting it for the first time, I should
be considered to be a senseless crank. "What a
funny idea!" you can imagine people saying.
"Fancy buying and selling things by handing
round the privilege of being owed money by a
bank". Nevertheless, that is precisely how we do
buy and sell the majority of the goods and services
in the country. In the course of the slow development of banking people have come to have
confidence in the bank's promise to pay. My
I O U or yours is not accepted in payment for
goods and services. But the bank's I O U is
accepted. And for that reason the bank's I O U's
are *money*. Of course, the banker will not lend me
money unless he has reasonable security that I can
repay it. But that does not make any difference to
the fact that what he is lending is money. A
pawnbroker requires security before he will lend
you half a crown. But that does not make any
difference to the fact that the half-crown is money.

Not only are cheques money, they are the greater part of the money we have in this country. At present there is in this country about £70 million worth of coins, copper and silver, in the hands of the public, and about £420 million worth of Bank of England notes. But the money which the banks owe to the public, and on which the public can draw cheques, amounts to just over £2000 millions. This form of "bank money" is therefore four-fifths of all the money in existence in the country.

Now, there is room for endless dispute in discussing this interesting fact. Unfortunately I cannot give it more than a few pages, so I will just pick out a few objections that are sometimes urged against the system, and say a few words about each of them. First of all, let us go back to the imaginary visit I paid to the bank to borrow £100. Now suppose I *had* wanted £100 in actual hard cash. Obviously the banker could not have lent it to me unless he had it in his safe. But, in point of fact, what I wanted—and what everybody who borrows from the banks wants—was not hard cash, but merely a debt owing to me by the bank (what the banker calls a deposit); not hard cash at all, but merely an entry in his books. Now, clearly the banker doesn't need to have £100 in cash in his safe before he undertakes to owe me £100. In fact, he knows by experience that of all the money he undertakes to owe, only a very small proportion will ever be wanted in cash. British bankers work on the principle that if they have cash enough in hand to pay one-tenth of their debts they are all right. And, indeed, even that small fraction of one-tenth is more than is ever needed. Now this means that they can undertake many more debts than they have cash to meet. But their debts, being generally acceptable, are money. What happens, in effect, therefore, is that the banks can create money merely by making entries in their ledgers. That is rather a blunt statement to which there are all sorts of qualifications. I have space to deal with only one of them. Banks can create money in this way only so long as they retain the confidence of the public. So long as everybody believes that he *could* get cash—that is, coins and notes—out of the bank, nobody will want it. But if people start having doubts they will come round to the bank and start drawing out their deposits in cash. Now if that happens, the banker's 10 per cent reserve is quite inadequate. The first 10 per cent of the depositors will get their deposits in cash. But if the depositors still continue to run round to the banks for cash, the banker will have to ask for repayment from all the people to whom he has made loans. But it is utterly impossible for the banks to pay off *all* their debts in cash. In this country at present, for example, the banks have debts which amount to four times as much as the whole of the coins and bank-notes in existence. If a time arrives when the banker cannot scrape together any more cash from anywhere, then he has to close his doors. The bank has failed. It is a long time since we have had a run on the banks or a bank failure in this country. But it might happen again, and the prudent banker must always bear the possibility of a run in mind as one of the limitations on his power to create money.

There are other limitations on his power of creation which I have no space to discuss now, because I want to pass on to a fundamental question.

Is it right that anybody should be allowed to create money? And if I may give you part of the answer to that question I should say, "No, it is obviously wrong that anybody should be allowed to create money without control or limit". But in point of fact the banks do *not* create money without control or limit. They are subject to a very definite control exercised by the Bank of England, and the Bank of England itself is limited by the Acts of Parliament which define its powers. One of the subjects with which I shall be dealing in the next chapter is the question of the right amount of money to have in the country. But I suggest, in anticipation, that it is unlikely that we shall want the same amount of money at all times. If this is true, we must have some means of creating money when we want more or of destroying money when we have too much.

But should this power of creating or destroying money be in the hands of private institutions, or should it be reserved to the State? That, as you know, is a matter of hot political controversy. Apart from the rights and wrongs of the question, there is another aspect, which is perhaps not the least important. Would the job be done any better by the State than it is done at present by the banks?

Before we conclude this chapter, I should like once more to emphasise the fundamentally important fact about money. Money is of no value for itself. For example, take a penny, a £1 note and a cheque for £100. Of the three, the penny is itself the most valuable—that is, the metal in it is worth more than the paper in the £1 note or in the cheque. But none of the three would be of the least use on a desert island. Money's only purpose is as a ticket. A £1 note is fundamentally no more than a guarantee that says "The man who owns this piece of paper has contributed £1's worth of goods and services to the common pool and is therefore entitled to draw £1's worth out of it". It would be more accurate to say that that is what money *should* be. For it sometimes gets out of order and starts playing queer tricks. We must turn next to a discussion of some of those tricks.

9. SAVINGS AND CAPITAL

IT will be worth while, at the beginning of this chapter, to summarise very briefly the conclusions that were reached in the last. It was pointed out that the great bulk of our money to-day consists not of coins issued by the Mint, or of notes issued by the Bank of England under the authority of Acts of Parliament, but of cheques drawn upon the deposits in the banks. This can be explained by the nature of money. For money does not need to be coined from any very valuable substance, it does not even need an Act of Parliament to make it money. If people will accept cheques in payment for goods and services, then cheques are money. Anything that is generally acceptable is money, and if it became the custom to accept milk bottles or collar studs in payment for goods and services of all kinds, then milk bottles and collar studs would be money. A cheque is no more than an instruction to a bank to transfer a debt from one person to another. But because the general public has come to have confidence in cheques and to accept them readily, cheques have become money. Acceptability is the essential quality that money must have.

But if acceptability is the essential quality of money, its essential *purpose* is to serve as what the economists call a medium of exchange, an intermediary, a ticket. A piece of money, like a £1 note, is no more than a receipt for work done; it bears witness to the fact that its owner has contributed £1's worth to the common pool of goods and services and is entitled to draw £1's worth out of the pool. The £1 note is useless in itself; it merely serves as the intermediary between the contribution to the pool and the draft on the pool. That is not, of course, true of people, such as children or pensioners, who are given money without at the same time earning it. But they only get their incomes because they are given to them by somebody who *is* earning money. The origin of all incomes is in earning, that is, in contributions to the common pool.

That is as far as we got in the last chapter. The first question to ask in continuation of the discussion is, "How much money should we have? How many pounds' worth of receipts should the State have in existence?" Now from what I have just said, you might be tempted to answer that a receipt, a £1 note, should be issued whenever £1's worth is contributed to the pool, whenever, that is to say, £1's worth of work is done. But that is not so. Suppose, for instance, that you earn your living by making loaves of bread. Suppose that this week you have done £1's worth of work in making bread and that a brand new £1 note is printed and issued to you. Now the bread you have made will be consumed in a few days' time. But the £1 note will go on being handed round for a very long time. You may pay your rent with it, your landlord may use it to buy cigars, the cigar-merchant to pay his grocery bill, the grocer to take his family to the pictures, the cinema proprietor to buy petrol for his motor-car, and so on and so on. If a new £1 note were created every time any work were done there would very soon be far more £1 notes in existence than goods and services to buy with them. Goods are consumed, sooner or later (and most of them sooner), services can only be performed once. But money is almost indestructible; it can be used over and over again. One of the things that it is most essential to know —and at the same time most difficult to find out— is how many times a year the average piece of money is used. It is used fairly often for some purpose or other, for buying a newspaper or paying for a meal at a restaurant. But how often does the average piece of money form part of somebody's income? When a £1 note has been in somebody's pay envelope, how long is it until it gets into somebody else's pay envelope? We do not know exactly, but a pretty good guess would be once a month, or twelve times a year. I put that forward only as a guess, and indeed it is impossible to name any one figure. For the significant fact is that money gets handed round very much more quickly at some times than at others. And obviously when it is running round very quickly and getting into pay envelopes, say, twenty times a year, we need less money than at other times when it is moving more sluggishly.

So it is impossible to say how much money we need; it all depends on how rapidly money is being passed round. Let me illustrate that by the circumstances of Great Britain in the last five or six years. Less money is being put into pay envelopes now than in 1929—only very slightly less, but still it is a little less. There are slightly more men at work, but the average rate of wages has fallen a little. Now it would be possible to argue—some people *do* argue—that less money is being put into pay envelopes because there is less money to put into them. But that is not so. We have over £200 millions more money in the country now than in 1929. Whatever else we may be suffering from, it is not a shortage of money. What *is* happening is that the money we have is not passing round from hand to hand as quickly as it might do. If creating more money could make a nation prosperous, then we ought to be quite prosperous by now. Nobody would deny that the amount of money in existence is an important factor. But the experience of Great Britain in the last six years suggests, in my opinion, that there must be other factors that are much more important.

So I come back to the main question that we must ask ourselves. What part does money play in the economic system? In particular, what part does it play in upsetting things and producing depressions? It would be very pleasant if those questions could be answered in one sentence. But unfortunately they can't, and I shall have to ask you to accompany me into another round of explanations. Let us start at the beginning. How do we, you and I, get hold of money? Obviously by doing work of value, by contributing to the National Income. There are exceptions to that. Children, for instance, are given pennies without working for them. Pensioners have their incomes although they are *at present* contributing nothing to the National Income. But in both these cases, the children's pennies and the retired man's pension are not income from the national point of view, they are money that has had to come out of the earnings of other people. Generally speaking, it is true that money incomes can only be obtained by making some contribution to the National Income, to the common pool of goods and services. Now, as I have remarked before, some sorts of contribution, such as allowing your land to have factories built on it, are very much better paid than other sorts of contribution, such as risking your life in a coal-mine. That is true but, as I have also remarked before, it is for the moment beside the point. The point is that the miner's wage and the millionaire's income are both payments made for services rendered to the community, for goods or services contributed to the pool. Let us call this fact No. 1: All money incomes are given in return for contributions to the pool.

But the money does not grow on trees, it is given to us by somebody. And in the case of the vast majority of people it is given to us by an employer. Now, just consider for one minute the business of making bread. That business employs a vast number of different kinds of people. Bakers, shop assistants, millers, wheat farmers devote the whole of their time to making bread. Other people, such as railwaymen, coal-miners, iron and steel workers, engineers and a thousand others devote small fractions of their time to making bread. But whether they are whole-timers or part-timers in the bread business they all have to be paid, and the sum total of the money that is paid to them is the cost of the bread. That is a point that is not always realised. If a loaf of bread costs 4d., that means that four pennyworth of labour or of some other service has gone into that loaf. Now if you ask the baker, he will say that only part of that

4d. is labour, the rest is for flour and yeast and rent. But when he buys flour, he is only paying for the labour that has gone to produce the flour. Nobody pays money to a stalk of wheat or to a millstone. Money is only, in the last analysis, paid to men, because men are the only creatures who have any use for it. Rent is not paid to the house, but to a living landlord, who uses it for cigars and shirts and bus rides. Even the profit that the baker keeps for himself is his income, with which he buys his food and keeps his family. So this is fact No. 2: Income is income to the person who gets it, but it is a cost of production to the person who pays it out, and the total of all our incomes is the same thing as the total cost of producing all the goods and services that make up the National Income. If you want it in the form of a mathematical equation, Costs of Production = Incomes. I might say in passing that there are a number of qualifications to that statement—as, indeed, there are to all the statements I am now making—but they are all, in my opinion, minor qualifications which do not affect the main truth of what I am saying.

But if the system is to work properly, these goods that have been produced must be sold for a price that will cover their cost of production, including the usual rate of profit. Fact No. 3 is: Price = Cost of Production. Now let us put these

facts together. We all join in a co-operative effort
to produce the National Income. And in return
for our contributions we are paid money. Those
payments of money are the cost of producing the
National Income. But at the same time they are
the only source of money to buy the National
Income. And if the system is to work properly,
the money that was paid out to produce the
National Income must come back to buy it. You
can best visualise the whole business, perhaps, by
thinking of it as a circle. Industry pays out
money to its workers, the workers spend it on the
goods they want and so it gets back to industry.
The money of the community is continually chasing round this circle, appearing first as costs of
production when it is paid out by industry, then
appearing as income to the people who have made
the goods or performed the services, then acting
as their expenditure when they buy the necessaries
and luxuries they want, and so it gets back, in the
form of prices, to industry.

But if the system is to work properly, it is
essential that the same number of pieces of money
shall come back to industry as went out, neither
more nor less. Let us suppose, for example, that
while the money is chasing round the circle, the
banks suddenly create more money and put it into
the circle. Then more will come back to industry
than went out. There will be more money than

goods. More receipts for contributions to the pool than there are goods and services in the pool. That means that a few people, the people who have got the new money, will be able to get goods and services out of the pool without putting anything in, and in consequence everybody else will get less out than they put in. This is what happens when there is a sudden rise of prices. Everybody is working just as hard as before, but the rise of prices prevents them from buying with their incomes as much as they did before.

Now take the opposite case. Suppose less money comes back to industry than went out. Obviously some of the goods that have been made will not be sold and the people who have made them will be out of a job. Now you can see at a glance that this bears a strong resemblance to our present situation. There does not seem to be enough money coming forward to buy the goods that British industry could produce. Somehow, money is getting lost on its way round the circle. How is it getting lost?

Suppose I have £100 and I do not want at the moment to consume £100 worth of goods. I can simply keep my hundred £1 notes. The more £1 notes I have the richer I am. Any one of them can be used at any time to buy whatever I want, and meanwhile they serve me as a useful way of storing my wealth. But there is a very serious complication in this. My store of £1 notes makes me richer. But it doesn't make the community any richer. There are no more loaves of bread or suits of clothes or houses in existence because I have a few pieces of paper locked away in the money-box. Suppose every man, woman and child saved £10 between now and next midsummer. We should all consider ourselves to be £10 richer. But should we really all be any richer? In what way would we be any better off? We should not be able to produce any more bread or meat because of the saving. And meanwhile a great deal of bread and meat would have gone bad because we preferred to save our £10 rather than buy them. The individual can store wealth, can make himself richer, by piling up money; the community as a whole cannot. But the community as a whole is merely a collection of individuals. And if we all try to do as individuals what we cannot possibly succeed in doing as a community, there is bound to be trouble.

But is there any way in which the community as a whole can *store wealth*, can make itself richer? Obviously, there is. The community can make itself richer by turning some of its labour force on to the production of goods that will be useful in the future, such as houses, roads, bridges, canals, railways. Or else it can make machines that will increase its productive capacity in the future, like looms, or rolling-mills, or printing presses. In a

L

word, the community can enrich itself by making capital goods. Moreover, this is the only way that the community can enrich itself. We of the twentieth century live much more abundant material lives than our forefathers in the tenth century. It has been said that the poorest working man in 1935 lives better than the richest baron in 935. That change is due almost entirely to the fact that we were born into a world which was much more plentifully equipped with capital goods of all sorts —roads, houses, railways, ships, machines—than our forefathers' world was. It is our duty to maintain the capital we received from our fathers, to increase it, and to pass it on unimpaired to our children. Economic progress depends absolutely upon that.

Now the bearing of all this on the money problem is obvious. For when people save money they take it out of the circular stream of money. If nothing happened to bring it back again there would be less money coming back to industry than went out, with the usual result of falling prices, depression and unemployment. It is therefore vitally necessary to see that any money which is saved and taken out of the stream of money is put back into it again to buy capital goods which will enrich the community in the future. In other words, if savings are to do any good to the community, they must be given a concrete form, in

the shape of capital goods. In times of depression
there is more saving being done than capital goods
being produced. More money is taken out of the
circular stream than is put back into it. Consequently there is a shortage of purchasing power
to buy the goods industry can produce. In short,
we have the paradox of poverty in the midst of
plenty.

The difficulty of the whole business arises from
the fact that the people who do the saving are not
necessarily, in fact are not usually, the same people
as those who produce the capital goods. Who, for
example, are the savers? First of all, individual
rich men with more income than they can spend.
In the past, rich men have been the source of most
of the community's savings, but now they play a
very much smaller part than you might think.
A great deal of saving is done by poorer people by
means of institutions such as savings banks, thrift
clubs, building societies or life insurance societies.
But another part of our saving is not done by
individuals at all. It is done, for example, by companies which put some of their profits to reserve,
instead of paying them all out to their share-
holders. Or finally, saving can be done by the
Government. When, for example, the Government makes motorists pay a tax and then spends
part of the proceeds on making roads, it is for-
cing motorists to save. In one way or another, the

community saves about £400,000,000 a year—about one-tenth of its whole income.

But the people who make the capital goods or who buy the capital goods are often quite different people from those who do the saving. Sometimes they are the same. When a company puts £1000 to reserve and then spends that £1000 on a new machine, it is at one and the same time saving and buying capital goods. So is the Government when it levies a tax and spends it on a road. But these are the exceptions. The rule is that the person who saves does not buy capital goods with his savings and that the person who buys capital goods has not himself saved enough money to pay for them.

Is it any wonder, then, that savings and capital frequently get out of step? In the last few years, economists have been brought to believe that these irregular relations between savings and capital are at the root of the economic troubles that afflict the world. In fact, the importance of the subject must be my excuse for inflicting such a long abstract discourse upon you.

Well, what can we do about it? If savings and capital are always getting out of step with each other, what can we do to keep them in step? The answer is, unfortunately, so far as we know, very little. You can hardly order people to save more or less. You can hardly order them to produce more or fewer capital goods. All that you can do is to offer them an inducement, and the best inducement we have to offer them is that mysterious thing that keeps bobbing up in the newspapers, Bank Rate.

It is easy to see that the rate of interest has a great deal to do with saving. If you can get 10 per cent interest on your money, there is much more inducement to save than if you can only get 2 per cent. It is not quite so easy to see how the rate of interest affects the production of capital goods. But let me illustrate it by an example. Suppose you are thinking of building a £600 house and you ask the building society how much interest they would charge to lend you the money to build it with. If the rate of interest the building society charges is 8 per cent, your house will cost you about 18s. 6d. a week. If the building society charges only 4 per cent, your house will only cost 9s. 3d. a week. Obviously the lower the rate of interest, the readier you will be to build your house. Now, if there is more saving than capital production going on, the remedy is to lower Bank Rate, which will induce people to save less but to produce more capital goods. And similarly, if there is a shortage of saving the remedy is to put Bank Rate up. That is why in periods of depression you have low Bank Rate and so-called "cheap money".

But unfortunately there are many other factors that influence people in saving or in producing capital goods, and movements of Bank Rate often fail to produce any effect. Thus if people are frightened that a crisis is coming, they will be unwilling to bind themselves to buy a house, however low the rate of interest. But when you get a combination of increasing confidence in the future with cheap money, it may prove to be a powerful influence for the good. During the last $3\frac{1}{2}$ years, for example, we have had cheap money in this country, and though its influence is frequently exaggerated, nobody would deny that it has had a lot to do with our recovery.

But it is rather a roundabout method of controlling savings and capital to do it by moving the rate of interest up and down, and one of the most interesting speculations in the whole of economics is whether the State could exercise any more direct control. There is, for example, one school of thought which maintains that when insufficient capital goods are being produced, the State should step in and itself supervise the carrying-out of useful works of capital development, such as the building of roads, bridges and schools. A more ambitious plan is that the State should control the whole business of lending and borrowing money for capital purposes, with the object of seeing that the amount of capital development each year coincides with the savings that the community has available to finance it. But whatever the exact method, there are likely to be considerable advances in the immediate future in the direction of controlling the process by which the community increases its capital wealth.

10. FINANCING THE GOVERNMENT

Out of every £ of our income, 2s. 2d. goes in direct taxes. A direct tax is one for which you have to make a special payment directly to the Government, like income tax or death duties. When you pay income tax, you know that you are paying a tax; there is no possibility of being under any illusion about it. But there are also many indirect taxes. There is a tax on tea, on sugar, on beer, on spirits; there is even a tax nowadays on flour for making bread. But these taxes are all wrapped up in the price of the article. When you buy a packet of tea, the grocer doesn't say, "So much for the tea and 3d. extra for tax, please". But you are paying the tax nevertheless, even though you may never be aware of the fact. Moreover, there is another sort of tax that was not included in the 2s. 2d., and that is the rates that we pay on our houses. Some people pay their rates direct to the local council, and know that they are paying them, while for other people rates are included in rent. But, just as in the case of the tea duty, you pay it just the same, whether you know it or not. Taking all these taxes together—direct taxes, indirect taxes and local rates—they amount to something like 4s. 7d.

out of every £ of our income; very nearly a quarter.

Now this is a tremendous proportion. Almost one shilling out of every four we earn has to be paid over to the Government. Of course, that ratio is an average. We don't *all* pay over one shilling in four, and I shall have something to say in a minute or two about the amounts that the rich and the poor and the middle class have to pay in taxes. But, even as an average figure, one shilling in four is a very large proportion.

Some people frequently argue as if money paid in taxes was pure waste and served no economic purpose at all. If this is true, then it is a very serious state of affairs—we cannot afford to waste a quarter of our whole National Income. But is it true? What do we pay rates and taxes for? Do we get value for our money?

Some of the things we get for our rates and taxes are services of great value, which we should in any case have to provide in some way or another. We get the services of the police, for example, to keep the peace at home, and of the army, the navy and the air force to defend us abroad. We get a variety of essential services, such as sewage disposal and street-cleaning. We get the services of the teachers and of the Civil Servants who are necessary to run the machine. Now all these are useful services; they are all services that we have got to have anyhow. You pay for the service of

the tram conductor by buying a ticket whenever
you take a tram-ride. You pay for the services of
the policeman in your rates and taxes. But both of
them are performing useful and essential services,
and the different ways in which you pay for their
services does not make any difference to their use-
fulness or their value.

So all that part of rates and taxes which pays
for services of this kind is exactly on a par with all
the rest of your expenditure. It happens to be com-
pulsory expenditure, but that does not make it
any less valuable. But this is only a part—perhaps
only about a third—of the amount we pay in rates
and taxes. What happens to the rest? The remainder
goes in two different ways. Some of it goes in paying interest on the National Debt. And some goes
in the Social Services; that is, in housing subsidies, old-age pensions, unemployment insurance
benefit and assistance payments and so forth. In
brief, the Social Services can be defined as expenditure that is intended to benefit not the nation
in general, but specifically the comparatively
poor. Now, so far as the taxpayer is concerned,
the money spent on the National Debt and on
Social Services is a dead loss. The average taxpayer pays something like 3s. in every £ of his
income for the National Debt and the Social
Services. But unless he happens to own some War
Loan, or to be eligible for an old-age pension or

unemployment assistance or some other social service, he gets none of it back. But—and this is the point—*somebody* gets it back. The holder of War Loan, the elderly, the unemployed and the rest of them, do get it back in cash. The taxes that the taxpayer pays are transformed into the income of these other people.

None of the money we pay in rates and taxes, then, is lost or wasted; about one-third of it is spent on useful services; and the remaining two-thirds is transferred from the taxpayer's income to somebody else's income. None of it, or almost none of it, is lost to the community as a whole. But whether it is consumed or transferred, the portion of the National Income that passes through the hands of the Government is so large that it will be well worth our while to spend a little time examining the ways in which it is raised and expended. Let us look, first of all, at the Government's expenditure and then turn to taxation.

There have been great changes since the years before the war in the things on which the Government spends its revenue. The war left us with a heavy burden of war pensions and a very much heavier burden of the National Debt. But there have been other changes not connected with the war. The system of social services was in its infancy when the war broke out, and it has been extended very rapidly in the last fifteen years. The expenditure on unemployment alone is well over half the whole pre-war Budget. In 1913 taxes amounted to about 1s. 6d. in the £. They are now three times as high. Let us give just a brief glance at the different items.

First of all, defence and war pensions, on which the nation spends 10d. in the £ of its National Income. War pensions are, of course, an entirely new liability since the war. But on defence we have actually, in recent years, been spending a smaller fraction of our income than before the war. Then we were spending over 3 per cent on the Navy and the Army. In recent years we have kept the Air Force as well, and done it for less than 3 per cent. We are beginning to increase our armaments again, however, and the figure is almost certain to rise. From the economic point of view this expenditure is a sort of insurance-premium. We spend 3 per cent of our total income on an Army, a Navy and an Air Force—all of them quite useless in peace time—in order to be rather more secure in time of war. In a sense this is wasted money, but no more so than the money one spends on fire insurance. Unless we decide to get rid of the armed forces altogether, it is doubtful whether there is much possibility of substantial reduction in the amount of money we spend on them. Another part of the expenditure goes on the cost of government; that is, on the

cost of having buildings and a trained staff to perform all the jobs that have to be done to keep the
machinery of State moving. In short, the cost of
government is the cost of the Civil Service, including in that term not only the high and remote
officials who sit in Whitehall, but the much more
accessible officials of the local Labour Exchange,
and the constable upon his beat. On all this we
spend about $3\frac{1}{2}$d. in the £. The central Government in London also pays every year another sum,
also equal to about $3\frac{1}{2}$d. in the £, to the local
authorities to help them with their finances. And
there is also a tiny item of money spent on trade,
industry and agriculture. At present this only
amounts to $\frac{1}{2}$d. in the £, but, with all the subsidies
of recent years, it is increasing.

These things that I have mentioned already
roughly make up the services which we pay the
Government to perform for us. Taken all together
they cost us just short of 1s. 6d. in the £ of our
income, and they make up rather more than one-
third of the taxes that we pay to the central Government. They cost more than they did before the
war, but not very much. If we leave out war
pensions (which are costing less each year, in any
case) these Government services cost only about
3d. in the £ more than they did before the war.
Broadly speaking, I think we can say that we get
fair value for our money. Let us therefore pass on

to the more expensive and more controversial items, the Social Services and the National Debt.

The Social Services nowadays cost about £430 millions a year—that is, more than 10 per cent of the National Income. But not all this money comes out of the pocket of the taxpayer. Some of it is paid by the beneficiaries themselves. For example, almost the entire cost of health insurance is met by the contributions of the insured men and women and their employers, and a large part of the cost of unemployment insurance is also met by contributions. Secondly, large sums are provided by local authorities, especially for housing and poor relief, and these fall on the ratepayer rather than the taxpayer. But when all these allowances are made, the taxpayer finds the largest part of the cost of the Social Services. In 1932, the last year for which we have accurate figures, the taxpayer paid just about £190 millions for these purposes, the largest items being £80 millions for Unemployment, £40 millions for Old Age Pensions, £48 millions for Education and £14 millions for Housing. What is going to happen to these sums of money in the future? Are they going to increase or to decline? Is the burden of Social Services on the taxpayer going to be greater or less? We all hope that expenditure on unemployment and poor relief will decline as the number of unemployed persons gets smaller, but after the experience of the last fifteen years, it would be rash to make any predictions about it. But expenditure on Old Age Pensions will certainly increase as the number of elderly people increases. And as for expenditure on Education, Health and Housing, most people don't *want* to reduce it. So, taking them altogether, there is very little prospect of the Social Services costing us less in the future than they do now. They are much more likely to cost more.

So we come to the last big item, the National Debt, which is costing us something like £220 millions a year. As I pointed out earlier in this chapter, money paid in interest on the National Debt is not lost to the community: it is merely transferred from the taxpayer's pocket to the bondholder's pocket. The cost of the National Debt has been reduced quite substantially in the last few years. The biggest lump of the National Debt is the War Loan, on which interest used to have to be paid at the rate of 5 per cent each year. But in the great conversion scheme in the summer of 1932, the Government got its creditors' permission to pay no more than $3\frac{1}{2}$ per cent each year in future. Other loans have also been converted in the same way, with the result that the National Debt now costs about £100 millions a year less than it did ten years ago. That means to say that the taxpayers of the country, as a whole, are £100 millions a year better off than they would have been without those conversions, while the bondholders are £100 millions a year worse off. The nation as a whole is neither better off nor worse off, at least so far as the direct effects of the conversion are concerned, although the indirect effects of the conversion in lowering interest rates have, of course, been considerable.

Is the cost of the National Debt likely to rise or fall? We repay a little of it each year, which means a reduction of total cost, but the repayment is so slow that its effects cannot be distinguished. There is very little prospect of any further conversions to reduce the rate of interest. It used to be argued some years ago that instead of taxing people's incomes to pay interest on the National Debt, a very much larger tax should be put on their capital to pay off part of the principal of the Debt. But there are various technical difficulties in the way, and we do not hear very much about this so-called capital levy these days.

I have now mentioned all the chief items of expenditure. The miscellaneous services of Government are, on the whole, good value for the money. There is very little prospect of reducing them. Indeed, if we are going in for an increase in armaments, they will increase in cost. The Social Services we do not *want* to reduce in cost. And there is very little prospect of reducing any further the cost of the National Debt. So we can take it that the Government will go on spending at its present rate of about £700 millions a year, and, consequently, that £700 millions a year will have to be found in taxes. With that introduction, we can turn to have a brief look at the different sorts of taxes we pay.

There have been great changes in taxation, as well as in expenditure, in the last twenty-five years. There are perhaps fewer innovations and comparatively few brand-new taxes, but the increases in the existing taxes have been very large and very heavy. The chief dividing line between taxes is that between direct taxes and indirect taxes, which I have already mentioned. The three great direct taxes are the income tax, the surtax and the death duties, and they bring in just about half the total of the Budget. The other half comes from indirect taxes, of which the biggest are the taxes known as Customs and Excise. A customs duty is a tax imposed on goods coming into the country—such things as the tea and sugar duties, as well as all the protective tariffs that have been imposed in the last few years. An excise duty is a tax levied on goods that are made inside the country, such as beer and whisky. Taking the customs and excise duties together, the two biggest are the tobacco duty and the beer duty, which have been running a neck-and-neck race for first place in recent years. The petrol duty is a good third and the spirits duty fourth.

I have mentioned by name the three great direct taxes—income tax, surtax and death duties—and several of the most important indirect taxes, such as the beer, tobacco, petrol, tea and sugar duties. I have not been emphasising the distinction between direct and indirect taxes just for the fun of it, but because it is of some importance. In the case of a direct tax it is possible to make the tax vary in accordance with the taxpayer's ability to pay. If you have more income, you pay more income tax. And if you die and leave £1,000,000, your heirs will have to pay much more in death duties than if you only left them £1000. But with indirect taxes you can't do that nearly as well. A millionaire drinks very little, if any, more tea than a day labourer. Both of them pay about the same amount to the Government in tea duty. It may sometimes be that the poor man pays more tax than the rich. For example, the poor man eats more bread than the rich man. Now for the past three years there has been a tax on bread; it has been disguised under the name of a wheat levy, but it amounts in effect to a tax on bread, and of that tax it is likely that the poor man pays more than the rich man. This is not true of all indirect taxes. There are some—the tax on male servants, for example—which no poor person pays. There are others, like the whisky duty, which probably

THE NATIONAL BUDGET

REVENUE: £ MILLION

DIRECT TAXES (INCOME TAX, SURTAX, DEATH DUTIES)	367
INDIRECT TAXES - - -	314
MISCELLANEOUS - - -	44
	725

EXPENDITURE: £ MILLION

	NATIONAL DEBT - - -	225
ESSENTIAL SERVICES	COST OF GOVERMENT - -	42
	DEFENCE - - - -	108
	EDUCATION - - -	51
SOCIAL SERVICES	HEALTH & HOUSING - -	22
	LABOUR & UNEMPLOYMENT	76
	OLD AGE, ETC. PENSIONS	53
	WAR PENSIONS - -	45
	TRADE, INDUSTRY & AGRICULTURE -	9
	COST OF REVENUE COLLECTION -	12
	GRANTS TO LOCAL AUTHORITIES -	53
		696

THE BUDGET, 1933–34

affect the rich man more than the wage-earner. But, broadly speaking, the bulk of the indirect taxes comes from the pockets of the poor. Beer, tobacco, tea, sugar, matches—all these are things of which the poor man consumes pretty nearly as much as the rich man—and the five I have named contribute to the Government more than the death duties and the surtax put together.

The direct taxes then, are those whose burden falls mainly on the rich, while the indirect taxes are, in the main and with a number of qualifications and exceptions, those whose burden falls mainly on the poor. Now obviously the next step for me to take is to ask whether our system of taxes, as a whole, is fair as between rich and poor. But that involves first making sure what we mean by a fair system of taxation. It is fairly obvious that a rich man ought to pay more than a poor man. If you have two men, one with an income of £100 a year and the other with an income of £10,000 a year, it is obviously unfair to ask them to give exactly the same sum to the Government. If every inhabitant of the country were asked to make an equal contribution to the Government's expenditure, the contribution would work out at about £16 a year per head, or say 30s. a week for an average family of husband, wife and three children. There are some families that would never notice the loss of 30s. a week. And there are other

families who could not possibly afford to pay as
much as that to the Government. In short, a
system of equal contributions would be grossly
unfair. The rich man should therefore pay more
to the Government than the poor man.

Let us go back to our two men, one with an
income of £100 a year, the other with an income a
hundred times as large. Would it be fair if the rich
man paid a hundred times as much in taxes as the
poor man? Both of them would then be paying
the same proportion of his income to the Government. Now if each of us had to pay the same proportion of our incomes to the Government, the
proportion—taking rates and taxes together—
would be something like a quarter. So our £100
a year man would pay £25 and the £10,000 a
year man would pay £2500. Would that be
fair? I think obviously not. A man who can only
earn £2 a week has a hard enough time of it
making ends meet without taxation, and if you
made him hand over 10s. out of his two pounds,
it might mean actual starvation for him. But the
£10,000 a year man, though he might be paying
the enormous sum of £2500 in taxes, would still
have £7500 left, which would provide all the
luxury that he could decently desire. A system
of *equal contributions* is obviously unfair. A system
by which we all paid an *equal proportion* of our incomes is perhaps not quite so obviously wrong, but

it would be very unfair in practice. I think the only fair taxation system would be one under which the rich paid in taxes not only *more* than the poor, but a *larger proportion* of their incomes than the poor.

With this in mind, let us have a look at the British tax system. Now it is unfortunately impossible to say exactly how much in taxes anybody pays, because it depends on how much beer he drinks, how much tobacco he smokes and so forth. But it is possible to make some sort of guess, and the best guess that has been made was made by a Government Committee nearly ten years ago. And the result of their estimates was not very complimentary to the British system of taxation. They showed, for example, that a man with an income of £100 a year paid a higher proportion of his total income than a man with £1000 a year. It will surprise most people to be told that the class of people with the lowest burden of taxation are the middle classes; that is, the people with incomes of about £500 a year. We all know that our taxes press heavily on the very rich. But it is perhaps not always realised that they also press very heavily on the very poor. And there can be no doubt which of the two is in the better position to stand the heavy pressure.

This is not the sort of question on which it is possible to be dogmatic, but I think that anybody who looks into the matter carefully will come to the conclusion that our present system of taxation, owing to the heavy indirect taxes, places an unfair burden on the poor. Moreover, I have been talking only of taxes. Rates, which are a form of local taxes, also bear unfairly on the poor. They penalise the family man, who has to have a large house, more than the bachelor. They are heavier in poor towns than in rich towns, because the cost of poor relief is heavier. In fact, if you wanted to invent a tax which would be unfair in the greatest possible number of different ways, you couldn't do very much better than invent rates.

Now there are some people who would agree that our system of rates and taxes imposes an unfair burden on the poor, but who would argue that the poor get good value for it, for the poor are the only beneficiaries of the great system of Social Services that has been built up since the war. Now it is true the expenditure on Social Services is much greater now than before the war, and it is also true that all this money goes to the poor. But the increase in the expenditure on Social Services since 1914 is only just about the same as the increases in the taxes that the poor pay. It is true that if you are an old-age pensioner living in a subsidised house, who never drinks or smokes or travels in a motor bus, you have gained more than you have lost in the last twenty-five years. But if you are an ordinary wage-earner, who drinks a little and smokes a little, and who is drawing neither a pension nor health insurance benefit nor the dole, you have lost more in increased taxes than you have gained in Social Services. The working class as a whole has neither gained nor lost very much.

We all of us have one particular tax we dislike. If you are a rich man you probably dislike the death duties most of all. If you are a poor man it might be the beer duty or the tobacco duty. But it is no good merely saying, "Such-and-such a tax ought to be abolished". Somehow, by some means, the Chancellor of the Exchequer has to raise £700 millions a year. He could abolish the death duties, but he would have to put something in their place. He could do away with the beer and tobacco duties, but he would have to find some other way of raising the £120 millions that they now bring in. Don't let me stop you from disliking any particular tax. But if you say, "It ought to be abolished", that is only half a thought. What you ought to say is, "It ought to be abolished and such-and-such a tax put in its place". And if you think about it in that way you will probably come to the conclusion that it is unfortunately very difficult to see how any of our taxes could be abolished.

11. INTERNATIONAL FINANCE

THERE is something mysterious and forbidding, almost sinister, about the words, "International Finance". The international financier has become the bogey-man of the modern world and any economic catastrophe that cannot otherwise be explained is freely ascribed to his machinations. I think this popular belief is at least partly due to the difficulty and the natural obscurity of the subject of international finance rather than to any outstanding wickedness on the part of its practitioners. But it is worth making an effort to understand international finance, difficult though the subject is, because of its very great importance, not only to the nation as a whole but to each one of us individually. To remind you of the importance of the subject I need only recall to your minds the crisis of 1931. One school of thought says that that crisis was due to a plot on the part of international bankers to get rid of the Labour Government. The other school of thought says that the crisis was a reflection of the fact that Great Britain was caught in the great world depression and that it had become necessary to save the pound. But the only thing on which both sides are agreed is that the crisis was connected in one way or another with international finance. In such ways does international finance affect the personal lives of every one of us.

I can best make a start with the subject of this chapter by recalling to you two earlier chapters of this book. The first of these was the chapter on Foreign Trade, in which I discussed the importance to our whole economic structure of the trade we do with overseas countries. It was there estimated that one-sixth of all our working population earns its living by making goods for export. Indeed, if the unemployed were counted in too, the proportion would be more like a quarter. These export industries are the most depressed in the whole country; their homes are the distressed areas. Foreign trade is vitally important to the production of the National Income. And it is even more vitally important to the problem of unemployment.

The second chapter to which I should like to refer you is that in which I tried to explain the nature of money. I made the point in that chapter that the essential quality of money is its acceptability. Anything which people agree to treat as money is money, whether the law says so or not. Throughout most of the world's history, metal coins have been the most acceptable form of money. But in twentieth-century Britain we use metal

coins only for our smaller purchases, and even
then the coins are worth much more as money
than as metal. If you melt a shilling down, for
instance, the silver you will get will be worth much
less than a shilling. A shilling is really only a note
that has been printed on silver instead of on paper.
The forms of money which are most acceptable to
us to-day, and therefore most used, are bank-notes
and cheques. But—and this is the important
point—they are acceptable only in this country.
You can't buy things in one country with the
money of another country. If you don't believe
me, try to buy a packet of cigarettes with a
French bank-note. It will not be accepted by the
tobacconist. French bank-notes are not money in
England; they are merely coloured pieces of paper,
which have some value somewhere else, but no
value as money in England.

This fact makes it necessary to have a special
means of paying for foreign trade. Consider the
case of a British merchant who sells American
alarm-clocks. He sells them for British money,
British half-crowns, or £1 notes, or cheques drawn
on British banks. But half-crowns and £1 notes
are no use to the American workmen who made
those alarm-clocks. They want to be paid in dollars,
and if they don't get dollars they will want to know
the reason why. Or take the case of a British coal-
mine selling coal to Spain. The coal is sold in

Spain for pesetas. But the miners in South Wales want to be paid in shillings and pence. To get over difficulties of this sort there has to be some way by which pounds can be exchanged for dollars and pesetas for shillings.

Now I am not going to go into any of the technicalities of the foreign exchanges. There are plenty of books in which you can find them, and they are very dull in any case. But there are just one or two points which it is necessary to mention in order to get an idea of the way in which the system works. The first is this—that the process by which one country's money is turned into another country's money is one of *exchange*. There is no magic formula which turns a £1 note into five dollar notes. There is no machine that takes shillings in at one end and turns German marks out at the other end. If you have some pounds and you want some dollars, the only way to do it is to *exchange* them with somebody. What the City calls the foreign-exchange market is really a gigantic swapping match.

One of the consequences of this is very interesting and important. An exchange needs two parties. If I exchange pounds for dollars, then somebody else must at the same time have exchanged dollars for pounds. We need every year a large amount of foreign money to pay for all the foodstuffs and raw materials and manufactured goods which we buy from abroad. They must be paid for in foreign money, because British pounds are useless to the foreigner who has supplied these goods. And the only way we can get hold of foreign money is by swapping our pounds for it. But if pounds are useless to foreigners, why are they willing to give their own money in exchange for them? The answer is that they want pounds because they have payments to make in Great Britain.

You must therefore think of two sets of people: Englishmen wanting foreign moneys to pay for the goods they have brought from abroad, and foreigners wanting English money to pay for the goods they have bought from England or to make any other payments they may owe in England. These two sets of people swap their moneys for each other in the foreign-exchange market. It all sounds very learned, but it is really just the same as schoolboys swapping penknives for conkers. A penknife may at one time be worth five conkers, but later in the season it may be worth as many as ten conkers. In just the same way the rate of exchange, as it is called, between different moneys varies from time to time. In the last four years, for instance, one pound has sometimes been worth less than $3\frac{1}{2}$ American dollars and sometimes as much as $5\frac{1}{2}$ American dollars.

It will be helpful to keep this picture of a

swapping match in mind because it will help to keep you from going astray later. You often hear people say that it is unpatriotic to buy foreign goods, because to do so sends money out of the country. Now a second's thought will show you that that is nonsense. If you buy, let us say, an American motor-car, your pounds get as far as the grand swapping match in London, where they come into the possession of somebody else. But whoever that somebody else may be, and whatever may be the purpose for which he has acquired your pounds, one thing is certain: they will not go out of the country. And for a very good reason, because once a £1 note gets outside this country it is valueless. Nobody wants pounds except to spend them in Great Britain. There may be any number of other reasons why you should "Buy British", but this is not one of them. Whether you buy British or foreign, the money you pay will continue to circulate in this country, the only place where it has any value.

I have just been saying that the only way in which we can make payments to foreigners is by exchanging our pounds for their foreign moneys. And the only way they can make payments to us is by exchanging their foreign moneys for our pounds. It follows that the number of pounds we give away in the exchange is exactly the same as the number of pounds the foreigners get in the exchange. That is pure common sense. The number of penknives lost by swapping must be the same as the number of penknives obtained by swapping. That means that *the payments we make to foreigners must be equal to the payments we receive from foreigners.* They must be equal at all times and in all conditions—not because of any learned law of economics, but because of the ordinary common sense of swapping: the number of pounds *given* in exchange must be the same as the number of pounds *taken* in exchange.

Let us take a brief look at the payments made to foreigners by this country and the payments made by foreigners to this country; those are cumbrous phrases, so let us talk about out-payments and in-payments, meaning payments going out of this country and payments coming into this country. Much the greatest of all the out-payments of Great Britain is for goods imported. In 1934 we bought goods from abroad to the value of £742 millions; most of them foodstuffs and raw materials, but a great many other things as well. And in 1934 this payment for imports was about the only out-payment Great Britain had to make. In other years we have made War Debt payments to the United States, but they have now come to an end. There are also one or two trifling little sums; for example, we have to buy foreign moneys to support our Ambassadors and Consuls in foreign countries. But these are very small. Broadly speaking, imports of goods can be taken as the only things for which Great Britain in 1934 had to pay foreign countries. We had to go into the exchange market and offer £742 millions of our money in exchange for foreign money. And foreigners would only want that £742 millions if they had payments to make in Great Britain. So let us now turn to the payments they had to make, the in-payments.

Much the largest item, once again, is payment for goods. In 1934 we sold £447 millions of goods to foreigners—(and I might remark parenthetically that I am using foreigners here to include the Dominions and Colonies and I hope I shall be forgiven for doing so). That £447 millions accounts for 60 per cent of our out-payments; 60 per cent of our purchases of foreign goods were paid for, that is to say, by sales of British goods. But what about the other 40 per cent, the other £295 millions? Well, first of all, foreigners wanted a certain amount of British money to pay for the services of British ships. Our merchant marine, as you know, does more than carry our own trade, it carries a fair part of the trade of the rest of the world as well, and in 1934, according to the official estimate, foreigners had to pay £70 millions for British shipping services. And to make the payment they had to get hold of British pounds. There are other ways in which British people perform services for foreigners. A great deal of the world's insurance is done in London and foreigners have to have British pounds to pay the premiums. London is still in many ways the world's banker, and earns a considerable sum in fees and commissions on business done for foreigners. These, and a great variety of other services performed for foreigners, are estimated to have brought in £50 millions in 1934. Together with the earnings of our merchant marine they make £120 millions. So 60 per cent of our imports are paid for by sales of goods, and another 16 per cent by sales of services. But that still leaves 24 per cent, or £175 millions, unaccounted for. What other payments did foreigners have to make to Great Britain? The answer is that they had to make interest payments on the money lent to them in the past by Great Britain. For a hundred years we have lent vast sums to foreign countries and to the Dominions and Colonies. Sometimes we have made direct loans to the foreign or colonial governments. Sometimes we have bought stocks and shares in foreign companies; this is particularly true, for example, of the United States, where British investors have a very great deal of money invested. Or sometimes we have merely built up a business in a foreign country, as for example, the British-owned railways in Argentina and many

N

scores of enterprises in the Dominions or Colonies. But whether you call it interest or dividends or profits, all this money has to be exchanged from the foreign moneys in which it was earned into British pounds. In 1934 this just made up the missing 24 per cent. Indeed, this will give you some idea of the magnitude of our foreign investments, for the interest on them was sufficient to pay for a quarter of all our imports.

The figures don't always come out quite as neatly as they did in 1934. Take 1929, for instance, the last year before the world crisis. In that year we bought £1220 millions of goods from abroad. But when you add up the value of our exports in that year, the value of the services we performed for foreigners and the interest and dividends on our foreign investments, it comes to £1323 millions, or £103 millions *more* than our imports. How could that be? How could we have in-payments of £103 millions more than our out-payments? The answer is that we could not and did not. British people were willing to put up £1220 millions to pay for their imports, and foreigners could get hold of that many pounds, and use them to make their in-payments, by offering their own money in exchange. But they couldn't get any more, because Englishmen would not offer any more, since they had no need of any more foreign money once they had paid for their imports. So the extra £103 millions had to stay abroad. It was handed over to Englishmen, but in foreign money, and the Englishmen had to leave it abroad, willy-nilly. In other words, Great Britain's foreign investments increased during 1929 by £103 millions. That sum was lent to foreigners. And we have been lending similar sums to foreigners almost every year for a century or more. The war years were exceptions and the coal-strike year of 1926 and the last few years of world crisis. But apart from that we regularly lend money to the Empire and to foreign countries. Since the war we must have lent something like £1000 million or even more.

Now, lending to foreigners is frequently subject to criticism, so it will be as well if I say a word or two about it. Let us take its good points first. The interest and dividends we receive on our past loans are of powerful assistance to us in paying for our imports of food and raw materials. In effect, we, as a nation, get a quarter of our imports free. Now, you might say that that is a very mixed blessing. If we didn't get a quarter of our imports free there might be more work for our depressed export industries in paying for them. But that is true only if there is unemployment, and even then only for a short period. We don't want, as a nation, to work any harder than we have to, and if we can get anything free we surely ought to take it.

A second ground of objection to foreign loans is that they are wasteful. Many people have alleged that foreign debtors default on their debts much more often than debtors at home, with the result that a large part of the money we invest abroad is lost. But I think this is very greatly exaggerated. Even in recent depression years the average rate of interest on all our foreign investments appears to have been about 4 per cent per annum, which is not by any means a bad figure.

It is also frequently said that loans to foreigners are bad because they enable foreign countries to develop their own industries and do without British goods. But, as I showed in the chapter on foreign trade, rich, developed and industrialised countries are, in fact, much better customers for British industry than poor, undeveloped agricultural countries. If British capital is opening up the undeveloped regions of the earth it is opening up markets for British industry.

It is a much more valid objection, in my opinion, that loans to foreigners frequently deprive British industry at home of the capital that it requires. That has undoubtedly happened in several years since the war. But it does not necessarily happen every year, and it would be wrong to condemn all foreign loans because they have sometimes been carried to excess. On balance, therefore, I think the arguments are in favour of foreign lending. But there is one overriding argument which, to my mind, settles the matter. Foreign loans are inevitable. Take the year 1929, for example. What could we do with that extra £103 millions except lend it to foreigners? We could have taken it in gold, but gold is not nearly as useful as foreign investments. We could have taken it in foreign goods, but we had already imported as many as we wanted. Or, if we had cut down our exports, there would not have been any £103 millions left over. But, with the export trades depressed, cutting down exports was the last thing we wanted to do. In the circumstances there was nothing we could do with that £103 millions except to lend it to foreigners. And those circumstances will recur in the future, so we might as well make up our minds to a continuance of foreign lending as soon as the present world crisis is past.

There are many aspects of international finance that I wish I had space to go into. But I have space for only one. And that one must obviously be the gold standard.

Perhaps I ought first to try to explain what the gold standard is. We have been discussing in this chapter the business of exchanging moneys for each other, and I mentioned in passing that the rates of exchange, that is, the ratios or proportions in which moneys exchange for each other, vary considerably from time to time. But these variations are bad for trade. Suppose, for example, you are trying to sell Belfast linen in the United States. The cost of production of the linen was in pounds. But you have got to sell it for dollars and you will obviously not know what price to ask for it if you do not know from one day to the next how many dollars exchange for £1. The gold standard is a device for preventing these variations. Nobody ever sat down and invented the gold standard. Like Topsy, it just growed. But its effect is as if the nations had met in conference and agreed that their moneys should each be kept equal in value to a given amount of gold. The pound, for instance when we were on the gold standard, was always worth just over $\frac{1}{4}$ oz. of fine gold. The American dollar was worth something like $\frac{1}{20}$ oz. of fine gold. Now Euclid, as you remember, said that when two things are each equal to a third thing, they are equal to each other. If £1 and 5 American dollars are each equal in value to $\frac{1}{4}$ oz. of gold, then £1 is worth 5 dollars. (It wasn't actually 5 dollars, but about $4\frac{7}{8}$, but 5 is near enough for our purposes.) And how, you may ask, was the pound to be kept equal in value to $\frac{1}{4}$ oz. of gold? By a very simple device. The Bank of England was ordered by Act of Parliament to buy any gold that was offered to it at £1 for $\frac{1}{4}$ oz. (the actual figure was 19s. $5\frac{1}{4}$d., but once again £1 is near enough) and to sell gold to anybody who asked for it at the same

price. Now nobody would be silly enough to pay
more than £1 for $\frac{1}{4}$ oz. of gold, if he could get it
for £1 at the Bank of England. And similarly
nobody would take less than £1 for $\frac{1}{4}$ oz. of gold if
he could get £1 for it at the Bank. So by this device
the price of gold was always £1 for $\frac{1}{4}$ oz., and so
long as other countries made and kept to similar
arrangements for their own moneys, the different
moneys would always be worth the same fractions
of each other.

But this system would work only so long as one
condition was observed. The Bank of England
could go on buying and selling gold only so long
as it had the gold to buy and sell. And that meant
that the whole policy of the Bank of England had
to be directed to the preservation of its gold reserve. So long as we were on the gold standard,
the Bank of England could not pursue the monetary policy that would be best for British industry
if that policy would endanger the gold reserve. That
is what happened between 1925 and 1931, when,
in order to keep its gold reserve, the Bank of
England had to keep Bank Rate much higher than
was convenient for British industry. Since we left
the gold standard, four years ago, the Bank has
been able to lower Bank Rate to the lowest level
it has ever reached, and to keep it there for longer
than ever before, with very beneficial results to
British industry.

Should we go back to the gold standard? If not now, should we look forward to going back to it later on? It is very difficult to answer those questions. When the exchange rates are continually jumping up and down, as they have been in the past four years, it is undoubtedly unsettling to foreign trade. British prosperity has been very largely built up on foreign trade. In particular, our export trades are the most depressed of all and we should do whatever we can to help them. Looking at the problem from that point of view, we undoubtedly ought to go back on to the gold standard.

But going back on to the gold standard may mean imposing a handicap on all our domestic industries, it may mean the end of the cheap money that has been largely responsible for the promising recovery of the last three years. Looking at it from that angle, we certainly ought not to go back to the gold standard.

Well, that is the problem. I wish I knew how to solve it. If we don't go back to the gold standard there is the dismal certainty of continued severe depression in about a quarter of our industries. If we *do* go back to the gold standard there is the possibility of a depression—less severe, it is true, but still a depression—in three-quarters of our industries. Which is worse: severe depression in a quarter of our industries with prosperity in the

rest, or moderate depression all round? Make
your own choice. And when you have made it you
will know whether we ought to go back on to the
gold standard or not.

12. KEEPING THE MACHINE GOING

In the previous chapters of this book an attempt has been made to describe the vast complicated organisation in which we all co-operate to produce the National Income, to distribute it and consume it. We have described in what different ways the people of these islands earn their livings, the industries and the places in which they do their work. We have discussed the special problem of foreign trade and have touched upon one or two of the problems that arise in connection with the supply of goods to the consumer. We have examined the way in which the National Income is shared out between different people and the way in which people spend their incomes. And, lastly, we have discussed the money system in many of its aspects, and especially in its relation to the question of savings and capital.

Throughout all these discussions I have tried neither to attack nor to defend the existing system. I have not said that it is the best possible, nor have I said that any other system would be better. I do not think it is my job in this book to express an opinion on that question; my job is merely to give the facts on which you can yourselves come to a decision. But nobody could possibly write 191 pages about the economic system, or even 191 lines, without admitting that the system is working very imperfectly, and I have certainly made no attempt to conceal its imperfections. And so I am going to devote the remaining pages to an attempt to explain, or, if I cannot explain, at least to discuss, why it is that the system works better at some times than at others, and why, in particular, it has been working so imperfectly in Great Britain since the war.

But before we begin that discussion, two words of warning may not be out of place. The first is a warning against exaggerating the defects of the existing system. It is true that at times we have booms and at times we have slumps, but the difference between the two is less than you might think. It would be difficult to say exactly what would be 100 per cent efficiency in the economic system. Perhaps the nearest approach would be to say that that economic system would be 100 per cent efficient which would always provide useful work for everybody who wanted to work. We should then be producing and consuming just as many goods and services as could be produced with the resources we chose to make available. There would be as much leisure as we chose to take, but no poverty-stricken unemployment. Now, judged by that criterion, our present economic system almost never falls below 75 per cent efficiency. Even at the worst times we are employing three-quarters of the available people. Three men out of four, even at the worst times, are actually engaged in producing the pool of goods and services by which we all live. That is really a comparatively small margin of inefficiency. If you could turn out a steam engine or a motor-car engine whose efficiency never fell below 75 per cent of its maximum, you would be doing pretty well. Now the difference between 75 per cent and 100 per cent may mean the difference between starvation and sufficiency for millions of families. I have not the least desire in the world to underrate the misery caused by trade depression. But in our concern for the misery it suffers to exist, let us not exaggerate. It is nonsense to talk about the present system breaking down. It has not broken down and it is not breaking down. It has no more broken down than a car has broken down when one cylinder ceases firing. It is running badly—yes; but broken down—no.

And the second warning that I think it is worth while to bear in mind is this: because our present system is working badly it does not necessarily follow that another system would work any better. It might, of course, work better, but you haven't proved your case when you point out the defects of the present system. You may remember that at the beginning of the book I expressed the three qualities we demand of an economic system as Efficiency, Adaptability and Equity: Efficiency in producing goods; Adaptability in adjusting itself to changing circumstances; Equity in sharing out fairly the goods and services available for consumption. Our present system falls short on all three requirements; shorter on some than on others. It may be that another system would be better; but it needs proving.

With those parenthetic remarks out of the way we can come back to our main subject. Why is it that trade is better in some years than in others? These alternations of good and bad are very peculiar. For one thing they come quite regularly. If you draw a curve of good and bad trade, you will find it goes up and down quite regularly. There is a boom every seven to ten years and a depression in between. For examples we can go right back to the fifties of last century. 1853 was the height of one boom, then it was seven years to the next in 1860, then five years to 1865, then seven years to 1872, then ten years to 1882—and so on and so on. Since the war there have been special influences working in England, and our booms have been merely a shade lighter depression than the surrounding years. But still this regularity persists. It was nine years from one comparatively good year (1920), to another peak (1929), and the experts seem to think that the next peak will come in 1937, about eight years after 1929. And in between each peak—whether the peak is real prosperity or just less depression—there are slump years.

This regularity (it is usually called the trade cycle) is far too pronounced to be dismissed as a coincidence. It can't possibly just *happen* to turn out like that in so many countries and so many decades, in so many different varieties of circumstances. There must be some reason for it. What is the reason?

Literally hundreds of books have been written to answer that question and scores of theories propounded, all of them different and many of them contradictory. It is much the safest thing to say that we don't know what causes the trade cycle. Every year we add a little to our knowledge. Gradually what were previously only guesses convert themselves, through accumulated experience, into established facts. But on the fundamental question we know very little. I might compare it to our knowledge of the disease of cancer. There, too, we know quite a lot, but not nearly enough to control the disease. We know how it shows itself. and in what stages it runs its course. We know how to alleviate it temporarily in some cases. But for the fundamental cause of cancer, and for the fundamental cause of the trade cycle, we are still groping in the dark.

One thing, however, I think it is possible to state with some certainty. The actions of governments have very little to do with the trade cycle. And conversely, governments can apparently do very little to help a country out of a slump. There are, I know, one or two apparent exceptions to that. There have been one or two governments in the last few years whose policies have been, in appearance at least, highly successful. The policy pursued by the Australian Government is an excellent case in point. But I think if you examine each case carefully you will find that favourable circumstances played the largest part, and Government policy the smallest part, in bringing about some measure of recovery. Of course, you will never convince the politicians or the electorate of that. Every Government that happens to be in office while trade is improving pats itself on the back, and is patted on the back by the electors, for causing the recovery. Conversely, every Government that happens to be in office while a slump is developing gets turned out of office in disgrace.

For example, the last Labour Government happened to be in office during the two years of steepest decline in trade conditions, and though no rational person could accuse the Labour Government of having *caused* the slump, it was defeated at the General Election just as if it had done it on purpose. And similarly, the National Government formed in 1931, having had the good fortune to come into office at the very bottom of the slump, had the electoral advantage of improving trade. I hope you won't think I am showing political bias in giving these examples. If you do, let me restore the balance by a prophecy. In the General Election of 1935 the Conservative party probably had more luck than it deserved. But in the next election it will probably have less luck than it deserves. The indications are that the last two or three years of the life of this new Parliament will be years of declining trade. I can tell you now with the utmost assurance that that declining trade will not be the Government's fault. In fact, the Government will probably try to stop it. But it will suffer from it at the polls nevertheless.

It is possible that Governments will, in the course of time, improve their method of handling depressions. After all it is only a few years since the subject began to be systematically studied. It is only since the war that it has been generally accepted as the business of governments to concern themselves with the ups and downs of the economic system. We have made some progress. In particular we have learned many valuable lessons in the course of the present depression. And we may make much more progress in the next few years. But I would not be too optimistic about governments entirely curing the present alternation of boom and slump. Before they can do that there are three separate difficulties to be met. First, the Government must know when a slump is coming, and people are so incurably optimistic that they are never willing to admit that the improvement is ended. But even if they can make up their minds in time, the second difficulty is to know, and to agree upon, the correct remedy. And that is a very difficult thing in a democratic country, when you have scores of different schools of thought, each pressing its own remedy. But the third difficulty is the greatest of all. Suppose you are convinced that a slump is coming and that you know how to prevent it. The odds are that your remedy will damage somebody's interests; it may even run counter to the immediate wishes of a majority of the people. How then, in a democratic country, will you put it through? How will you persuade the people to take drastic and possibly painful action before the need for it is apparent to the man in the street? Before we submit ourselves to that sort of medicine we need to have very much more confidence in our economic doctors than we are likely to have for many decades to come.

But I don't want to overdo the pessimism. Instead of saying what we do *not* know about the trade cycle, let us turn to what we *do* know. We may not be able to say why a slump comes, but we do know *how* it comes.

Let us suppose that the whole community is actively at work; that we are in the middle of a period of prosperity—or perhaps I ought to say so-called prosperity; that everybody who is available for work is at work, with no more than the necessary minimum of unemployment due to people changing their jobs, etc. The economic engine, let us suppose, is firing on all six cylinders. What does that mean? It means that we are all busily at work producing the things we want to consume. Everything that is produced, in this ideal state, finds a ready market and is consumed.

The way in which a depression first shows itself is that there is a sudden drop in demand for certain kinds of goods and services. One month all the bricklayers of the country are employed— that means that people are buying houses. Next month there is suddenly a great reduction in the demand for houses, very few people will employ bricklayers, and large numbers of them are out of work. I have taken bricklayers purely as an example, and any other trade would do as well, though in point of fact the sudden disappearance of demand does usually show itself in industries like building, which produce capital goods.

This is the way in which all depressions start: a more or less sudden disappearance of demand in one or two industries. Sometimes a depression starts with a spectacular crisis on the Stock

Exchange or in the money market, as it did in the United States in 1929 or in England in most of the great depressions of the nineteenth century. At other times the depression does not herald its arrival so dramatically, but the trend of affairs just turns downwards. But in every case, dramatic or not, the first symptom is the disappearance of demand for the products of some industry, usually a capital-goods industry.

Once it has started, it is easy to see how a depression spreads. The bricklayers who have been thrown out of work have to cut down their household expenditure; they do not spend a penny more than they need to. And that, of course, throws more men out of work. The bacon they can no longer afford to buy, the tram-rides they cease to take, the shoes they cannot now buy—all these things provided jobs for other people. Now the bricklayers and their families do not entirely cease spending. They have to live, and whether it comes out of unemployment benefit or out of their own savings, they have to go on buying the bare minimum of essentials. So the jobs which depended on the bricklayers' spending do not entirely disappear. But they are substantially reduced. In the conditions of Great Britain at present, it is probably as near the truth as we can get to say that when one man is thrown out of work through a lack of demand for the products of his labour, the reduction of his expenditure and all the effects of his being thrown out of work result in a second man being thrown out of work. The final increase in the ranks of the unemployed is about double the number of those originally affected.

Let me illustrate that by some figures from our recent experience. In 1929 we had, in round figures, 1,000,000 unemployed. In 1930 and 1931, as a result of the lack of demand for our exports and for our capital goods, about another 800,000 men and women were thrown out of work. And the effect of these 800,000 coming off wages and going on to the dole put a further 800,000 out of work. So the total increase in unemployment was 1,600,000, which, added to the original 1,000,000, took the total to 2,600,000, which was very nearly the worst figure of the depression. Once more I must warn you not to take these figures too literally. They are roughly true, but I mention them more as an illustration than as statistics of precise accuracy.

It takes time, of course, for a depression to work itself out. Men are not always dismissed overnight, even when the demand for their labour disappears. The depression from which we are now slowly recovering took about three years from its start to its worst point. And the recovery comes in exactly the opposite way to the start of the depression. A time comes when the demand for some sort of goods starts to increase. Men are taken on, and the extra spending they can do as a result finds work for more men, and so the cumulative process starts working in the opposite direction. The depression was started in 1929, more than by any other single factor, by the disappearance of demand for our exports. And recovery was started in the autumn of 1932, more than by any other factor, by the sudden appearance of a large demand for new houses.

The conclusion to be drawn from all this is that if we want to find the cause of these ups and downs of trade, we must look for the causes of the increases and declines in demand for goods. What causes a sudden drop in demand—in spending—at one time and a sudden increase at another?

If you will cast your mind back to Chapters 8 and 9, you will be able to put your finger on one of the causes. These chapters were concerned with the monetary system, and they described the circular flow of money, continually being paid out by industry as wages, salaries, profits, dividends, etc., and continually coming back to industry to buy the goods and services produced. What we know as demand is nothing more nor less than this stream of money coming back to industry to purchase its wares. If anything happens to interrupt or diminish the stream, demand will fall, men will be thrown out of work and a depression will be on its way.

The saving, or hoarding, of money does act as an interruption of the stream, while the purchase of capital goods puts the money back into the stream. So if there is a sudden increase in saving, or a sudden fall in purchases of capital goods, a depression will be started. But that doesn't take us very much further in explaining *why* these sudden changes take place. Books have been written to elaborate explanations and I cannot possibly here go into all, or indeed into any, of the explanations. But the biggest reason—not the only one, but the biggest—seems to be a fundamental alternation in the human character between excessive optimism and excessive despair. At one time all sorts of rash ventures are undertaken. But when it proves that they were unsound and cannot pay there is a revulsion of feeling towards excessive pessimism, which, in turn, takes time to see its own foolishness. I fear this will seem excessively simple, almost simple-minded. But if you examine the most learned treatises on the subject you will find this same idea, wrapped up in more erudite language.

It is not always money which causes the alternation between boom and slump. Indeed, in a sense, it is never money, because money cannot think or act. When I wrote "money" I should have written "changes in human psychology showing themselves by altering the stream of money"— and it is not always those which cause depressions or booms. Sometimes the cause is much more simple. In Great Britain in 1929, for example, although money played some part, the biggest cause of the slump was the decline in the export trades. It would take me too far afield to try to explain just why that happened at that particular moment. But whatever the cause, it was outside Great Britain, and it would have happened whatever we did with our money. Sometimes booms start for similar non-monetary reasons. An important invention may open up a whole new field of demand. The development of railways about a hundred years ago, for example, stimulated an enormous demand for labour and materials and started several booms—although the thing people suddenly started to demand with such insistence was a thing they never knew they wanted before it was invented. Some people say that the invention of a cheap method of house-building will soon make us want to pull down our present houses and build new ones. It is possible—hardly likely perhaps, but possible—and if it happened it would without doubt stimulate a boom. When we have learned how to prevent these sudden ups and downs in the public's demand for goods and services, we shall have learned how to cure the trade cycle.

Now it must be obvious that this is far too large a problem to discuss in this book. So vast is this question of solving the mystery of boom and slump, that I cannot even claim in these pages to have given you more than a very sketchy notion of what the problem is. It is one of the most difficult in the world, both in theory and in practice, and one whose solution would contribute more to the material happiness of mankind than any other.

So I shall make no attempt even to begin a discussion of it in my last pages. But I should like to make one final suggestion, which applies not only to the subject we have been discussing in this chapter, but to the whole subject of national economics. We have been discussing in this book the economic system by which we earn our living. Some people consider that system to be marvellous. Others consider it to be unjust. But whether marvellous or unjust—and the system is both—everybody who studies it must admit that it is infinitely complicated. There is no simple solution for our economic woes. The economic system cannot be made perfect by any simple book-keeping, or by a handful of Acts of Parliament, or by printing paper money. I wish there were some simple solution, but there is not. The system can be improved; it must be improved. But if I have done nothing else in this book, I hope I have shown you some of the reasons why it cannot be brought to perfection in a week-end or a year or a decade or even a generation. Why, indeed, should anybody think that it is easier to understand, to control, to cure the infinite complexity of the social organism of two thousand million human beings, each of them moved by fear or habit or jealousy as often as by reason—easier to do that than to understand, shall we say, the workings of the human body? Yet nobody expects the doctors to make us all permanently and perfectly healthy between now and next week. Why should more be expected of the economists in their infinitely more difficult task? Their labour will be hard and fruitful and it will have its defeats as well as its victories. But though their progress may be slow, they can justly claim that they are working for the welfare of the human race with a devotion fully as great as that of the physician or the educator.

THE END

Printed in Great Britain by R. & R. Clark, Limited, *Edinburgh.*

WORKS ON ECONOMICS

WORKS ON ECONOMICS

THE GENERAL THEORY OF EMPLOY-
MENT, INTEREST AND MONEY. By
J. M. Keynes. 5s. net.

SOVIET MONEY AND FINANCE. By
L. E. Hubbard. 12s. 6d. net.

THE RUSSIAN FINANCIAL SYSTEM.
By W. B. Reddaway. 5s. net.

———

By G. D. H. Cole

PRINCIPLES OF ECONOMIC PLANNING
6s. net

STUDIES IN WORLD ECONOMICS
12s. 6d. net

ECONOMIC TRACTS FOR THE TIMES
7s. 6d. net

SOME RELATIONS BETWEEN
POLITICAL AND ECONOMIC THEORY
4s. 6d. net

MACMILLAN AND CO., LTD., LONDON